# the essential chocolate chip cookbook

recipes from the
classic cookie to mocha
chip meringue cake

by **elinor klivans**
photographs by kirsten strecker

**CHRONICLE BOOKS**
SAN FRANCISCO

To Jeff, my best friend forever

To the memory of our friend Larry Levitan, who lived his life to the fullest

Library of Congress Cataloging-in-Publication Data available.

ISBN-13: 978-0-8118-5804-5

Manufactured in China.

Designed by Azi Rad
Prop styling by Megan Hedgpeth
Food styling by Susan Sugarman

10 9 8 7 6 5 4 3 2 1

Chronicle Books LLC
680 Second Street
San Francisco, California 94107

www.chroniclebooks.com

## acknowledgments

Judith Weber, my agent, who makes it happen. A giant thank-you to the brilliant publishing team at Chronicle Books, especially Bill LeBlond, my editor, who is a great pleasure to work with, and Amy Treadwell, associate editor, who takes the absolute best care of my books. Bill and Amy make writing my books such fun. Kirsten Strecker, photographer, whose photos understand and illustrate the appeal and the fun of these desserts. Prop stylist Megan Hedgpeth and food stylist Susan Sugarmann, who took such care to make my desserts look exactly right. Judith Sutton, copy editor, who understands just what I am trying to say and makes it clear. My husband, Jeff, the chief taster, who always knows how to make it better. My daughter, Laura, the encourager, and my son-in-law, Michael, the listener. My son, Peter, and my daughter-in-law, Kate, who bake and cook together and truly enjoy chocolate and the chips. My grandchildren, Charlie, Madison, Max, Sadie, and Kip, who are already baking and decorating with chips. My mother, who baked my first chocolate chip cookie, and my father, who scoops the ice cream to go with the chocolate chip desserts.

Thank you to the chocolate chip testers who tested so many recipes: Jennifer Goldsmith, Melissa McDaniel, Rachel Ossakow, Dawn Ryan, Louise Shames, Kate Steinheimer, and Laura Williams.

A big thank-you to my circle of supporters and encouragers: Melanie Barnard, Flo Braker, Sue Chase, Susan Dunning, Natalie Dworken, Carole and Woody Emanuel, Barbara Fairchild, Rosalee and Chris Glass, Karen and Michael Good, Kat and Howard Grossman, Helen and Reg Hall, Carolyn and Ted Hoffman, Pam Jensen and Stephen Ross, Kristine Kidd, Alice and Norman Klivans, Susan Lasky, Robert Laurence, Rosie Levitan, Gordon Paine, Joan and Graham Phaup, Janet and Alan Roberts, Louise and Erv Shames, Barbara and Max Steinheimer, Kathy Stiefel, Elaine and Wil Wolfson, and Jeffrey Young.

# introduction

Ever since I tasted my first chocolate chip cookie, baked by my mother, I have been hooked on chocolate chips and any dessert that includes them. That chocolate chip cookie was the beginning of a lifetime spent preparing for this book. I have never tired of that original cookie, and I am always on the lookout for new ideas and creative ways to use chocolate chips. Check out the supermarket baking section and you will notice that the chocolate chip selection expands every year. There are a lot of other chocolate chip fans out there.

It is no surprise that so many of us love chocolate chips and chocolate chip desserts. A recipe that calls for a package of chips immediately seems familiar, comfortable, and doable. There are semisweet, bittersweet, milk, and white chocolate chips in various sizes that melt easily and eliminate having to chop chocolate. Chocolate chip ideas continue to spring forth. I use them in bars, cakes, pies, sauces, frostings, puddings, and muffins. Chocolate chips can add nuggets of chocolate to every bite of a chocolate cake, cheesecake bar, or crisp meringue. Melted or soft chocolate chips add a rich flavor to frostings, glazes, mousse, chocolate cream pie, and a hot brownie sundae cake. They make desserts better. When my agent, Judith Weber, said, "You are going to enjoy writing this book," she knew what she was talking about. I enjoyed every bite of testing (too much sometimes) and writing about a baking ingredient that I enjoy so much. From the Kitchen-Sink Chocolate Chip Cookies to the Chocolate Chip Cookie–Cookie Dough Ice Cream Bombe, this has been a sweet labor of chocolate chip love.

# all about chocolate chips

I have a very pleasant way to choose the brands of chocolate chips to use in my desserts: I taste them. I buy several kinds of semisweet, milk, and white chocolate chips and try each group separately. Talk about fun testing! A side-by-side tasting of chocolate chips will reveal that each brand of chocolate chips has its own unique flavor. What tastes best to me is the one I choose. I look for a strong flavor of chocolate, rather than sugar, to dominate. With white chocolate chips, I make sure cocoa butter is listed in the ingredients and I look for the subtle chocolate taste that cocoa butter lends. Some white chocolate chips are actually white chocolate coating and do not contain any cocoa butter. Below is a list of my favorite chips in order of preference.

### Semisweet chocolate chips
Guittard, Nestlé, Nestlé Dark, Hershey's Dark, Ghirardelli

### Miniature semisweet chocolate chips
Guittard, Nestlé

### Milk chocolate chips
Guittard, Ghirardelli

### White chocolate chips
Guittard, Barry Callebaut

### Miniature white chocolate chips
Barry Callebaut

### Bittersweet chocolate chips
Ghirardelli, Nestlé

Semisweet chocolate chips are available in regular and miniature sizes. A 12-ounce bag of semisweet chocolate chips, regular or miniature size, equals 2 cups. Bittersweet, milk, and white chocolate chips usually come only in regular size. Bags of bittersweet, milk, or white chocolate chips weigh only 11½ ounces but equal 2 cups. Regular-size chips are generally used for cookies, cakes, and pies. Miniature chocolate chips work well in frozen and creamy desserts and for studding a crumb crust with lots of bits of chocolate. Bittersweet chips have less sugar in proportion to chocolate and are a good choice for melting and for using in frostings, glazes, fudge sauces, and truffles. But none of these are hard-and-fast rules, just suggestions of what I find works best. If you are out of semisweet miniature chips, use the regular size. Bittersweet chips can always be substituted for semisweet.

Ghirardelli bittersweet chips are labeled as having a 60 percent chocolate content, and Nestlé bittersweet chips as having a 62 percent chocolate content. But for the remainder of chocolate chips made in the United States, companies keep their formulas secret and do not reveal the chocolate content. However, government guidelines require semisweet chocolate chips to have a chocolate content of at least 15 percent, and milk chocolate chips, 10 percent. To be labeled as white chocolate chips, chips must include cocoa butter. When a package is labeled "white chips," rather than "white chocolate chips," there is probably no cocoa butter in the chips.

Chocolate chips are best stored in a cool, dry place at between 60°F. and 75°F. for no longer than 3 months. Milk chocolate chips and white chocolate contain milk solids and are more perishable than dark chocolate chips; for these, 1 month is the limit. This all assumes that the chocolate chips were fresh when they were bought. A pantry or cabinet (not near the oven) is a good storage choice. Sometimes, especially in the heat of summer, you will see that a whitish film has formed on chocolate chips. This is chocolate "bloom" and results when chocolate chips have been stored at too high a temperature. Bloom does not affect the taste of the chocolate chips, and when they are used in baking, their good chocolate color returns. But if you meet me in my supermarket on a summer day, you will find me checking through the bags of chips to find those that do not have bloom.

Chocolate chips can be mixed into cookie doughs, stirred into pie fillings, or baked in cake batters. Lecithin, an emulsifier included in chocolate chips, helps them keep their shape. The unique shape of the chips also contributes to their retaining their shape when baked. Chunks of chocolate are more likely to melt into a cake and lose their identity, but chocolate chips remain whole and provide those soft, appealing same-size nuggets of chocolate in desserts.

However, chocolate chips melt easily and there is no need to chop chocolate. They are a perfect size for even melting. As is true for all chocolate, chocolate chips should be melted slowly and over gentle heat. Put the chocolate chips in a heatproof bowl or the top of a double boiler, set over a pan of barely simmering water, and stir until the chips are melted and smooth. Stirring helps the chips melt quickly and evenly. Depending on the quantity of chocolate chips, melting them will take from 3 to 5 minutes. Keep the heat low and reduce it if steam appears. As soon as the chocolate chips melt, remove them from the pan of hot water. Melted chocolate chips will firm up more quickly than cut-up chocolate as they cool and should be used within about 10 minutes. Combining chocolate chips with butter, cream, or oil both helps them melt smoothly and prevents them from firming up as quickly.

# notes on equipment and ingredients

*Below are details about the equipment used for these recipes and information for choosing the best ingredients.*

## equipment

These chocolate chip desserts cover many categories of baking, but the baking equipment they use is basic. If you do need to add a pan or utensil to your kitchen for one of these recipes, it will be one that is easy to find. Another option is to borrow a pan for a specific recipe: Mothers and friends are great sources.

Baking with good-quality pans that are the size called for in a recipe is key to baking success. Heavy pans bake evenly and do not warp after repeated use. An investment in good pans will pay off in years of successful baking. Shiny baking pans that reflect heat are less likely to produce overbaked cookie or cake bottoms than are dark baking pans that absorb rather than reflect heat. It is important to use pans of the right size. If the recipe says that cake layers should be baked in 9-inch round pans and you use 8-inch pans, the result can be quite different—and not to the good. The height of the pans is also important. Cake pans that have sides at least $1\frac{3}{4}$ inches, preferably 2 inches, high will prevent cake batter from spilling over the rim of the pan as the cake rises.

*Below is a list of the pans used in this book:*

| Type of Baking Pan | Pan Size |
|---|---|
| Baking sheets for cookies | Three 15-by-12-inch to 17-by-14-inch pans |
| Jelly-roll pan | One $15\frac{1}{2}$-by-$10\frac{1}{2}$-by-1-inch pan |
| Bundt pan or tube pan | One 12-cup-capacity pan |
| Loaf pan | One 9-by-5-by-3-inch (8-cup capacity) |
| Muffin tin | One tin with 12 cups |
| Pie pan | One 9-inch round pan |
| Round cake pans | Two 9-by-2-inch pans |
| Springform pan | One 9-by-3-inch and one 10-by-3-inch pan |
| Square baking pan | One 9-by-9-by-2-inch pan |
| Rectangular baking pan | One 13-by-9-by-2-inch pan |
| Tube pan with fixed bottom | One $9\frac{1}{2}$- or 10-inch pan at least $3\frac{3}{4}$ inches high |

### Double Boilers

A double boiler or a heatproof bowl that will fit snugly over a pan of hot water is essential for melting chocolate chips or beating cooked egg white frostings. Use a nonreactive container, such as stainless steel or heatproof ceramic, that will not discolor white chocolate.

### Electric Mixers

You can use a standing countertop electric mixer or a handheld electric mixer for any of these recipes. Electric mixers make beating easy, and handheld models are quite inexpensive. The frosting for the Chocolate Chip Angel Cake with Chocolate Marshmallow Frosting (page 94) must be beaten in a container over hot water, so a handheld mixer is the best tool for beating it.

### Parchment Paper and Aluminum Foil

Parchment paper, which comes in rolls or sheets, is the most practical choice for lining baking pans. Cakes and cookies can be removed in perfect condition, and cleanup is easy. Aluminum foil is another option.

## Miscellaneous Utensils

Graters are handy for grating citrus rind. Both Microplane graters and box graters work well. I prefer Microplane graters, which are patterned after a woodworker's rasp and make grating citrus rind a breeze. Have on hand several sets of measuring spoons, a set of dry measuring cups, and a liquid measuring cup. Dry measuring cups come in sets of four gradations, and I recommend buying the stronger metal ones over the plastic ones. For liquids, use cups with clear markings and place the measuring cup on a flat surface when measuring. A 2-cup liquid measuring cup is a good general size to have. A rolling pin is useful for crushing cookies into crumbs as well as for rolling out dough. Rubber, or preferably heatproof silicone, spatulas in several sizes are useful for folding mixtures together and for scraping the last bit of batter or frosting from a bowl. A strainer can do double duty as a strainer for various mixtures or fruit purees and as a flour sifter. For a regular flour sifter, I prefer one

with a rotary handle. A stainless steel sauce whisk is invaluable for whisking mixtures until smooth and for blending melted chocolate chips with whipped cream or other mixtures.

## Ovens

Knowing your oven is key to baking. Each oven has its own characteristics, and oven temperatures usually vary about 10 degrees within the oven, with the upper third and the rear of the oven usually being the warmest. If there is more than a 10-degree difference between an oven thermometer and your oven thermostat, or if your baked goods suddenly begin burning or underbaking during the normal baking period, the oven should be recalibrated by a professional. I am always careful to avoid overloading the oven, so the air can circulate properly. I bake one sheet of cookies at a time and find that they bake more evenly this way.

## Wire Racks

Cakes and cookies should be cooled on a wire rack. This allows for air circulation so that cookies remain

crisp and do not overbake on the hot cookie sheets, and cakes cool evenly and do not overbake. It is useful to have 2 racks.

## ingredients

All of the ingredients used for these desserts are readily available supermarket items. Many of them may already be in your refrigerator or pantry.

## Butter and Oil

I use unsalted butter in baking. This allows me to control the amount of salt that is added to baked goods. For recipes that use oil, I choose canola or corn oil.

## Citrus Zest

Citrus zest is the colored part of the rind of lemons, limes, and oranges. Rinse the fruit with warm water and dry it before grating the zest. Grate only the colored rind; the white pith under it is bitter. An average lemon yields about 3 tablespoons of juice and 2 teaspoons of zest; a lime yields about 2 tablespoons of juice and 1½ teaspoons of zest. A medium orange yields about ¼ cup of juice and 2 to 3 teaspoons of zest.

### Cream

Cream in cartons may be labeled whipping cream, heavy cream, or heavy whipping cream. Whipping cream has from 30 to 36 percent butterfat, and heavy cream and heavy whipping cream have from 36 to 40 percent butterfat. I used heavy whipping cream for these recipes. It whips up firmer and holds up longer than whipping cream.

An 8-ounce (½-pint) container of cream holds 1 cup, and a 16-ounce (pint) container holds 2 cups.

### Eggs

I use large eggs for all of my recipes. Eggs should always be stored in the refrigerator. Egg whites are sometimes separated from the yolks so that they can be whipped and the yolks and whites added separately to the recipe. It is easier to separate cold eggs. It is important to keep egg whites free of yolk since even a little yolk mixed in with egg whites will keep them from whipping (it is the fat in the yolk that interferes with the whipping). To separate eggs, have ready a small bowl for the yolks, a small bowl to break one white at a time into, and a large bowl to hold all of the egg whites. Crack the eggs one at a time, letting the white drip into the small bowl and putting the yolk in the other small bowl, then transfer the white into the large bowl. If a yolk breaks and mixes into the white, you will have lost only one white. Egg whites left over from a recipe can be sealed tightly in a clean grease-free plastic container and frozen for up to 3 months; be sure to label the container with the date and the number of egg whites. Defrost the still-covered egg whites overnight in the refrigerator. Extra egg yolks should be used immediately or discarded.

### Flavorings and Spices

Choose pure vanilla extract—made from vanilla beans, not artificial vanillin—and pure almond extract, which contains oil of bitter almond.

Store spices tightly covered, and replace stale ones. Spice storage times vary, but times are measured in months, not years. You can check spices by tasting a tiny bit to make sure that they are fresh and have a good flavor. I use kosher salt, which is free of preservatives. It is slightly coarse, but it does pass through my flour sifter and strainer.

### Flour

These recipes call for unbleached all-purpose flour or cake flour. Cake flour is fine-textured and makes an especially light cake. Cake flour is usually sold in 2-pound boxes. The two common brands found in the baking section of supermarkets come in bright red boxes that are easy to spot. I do not use self-rising cake flour.

### Leavening Agents

Baking soda, or sodium bicarbonate, is an alkaline leavening that must be combined with an acid ingredient, such as sour cream, molasses, or buttermilk, to activate it. As soon as it is mixed into a batter, the baking soda is activated and the batter should be baked promptly. Stored airtight, baking soda keeps indefinitely.

I use double-acting baking powder, which is the most common type. Double-acting baking powder contains baking soda (alkaline) and two acid ingredients, one of which is activated by liquid and the other by heat. Store baking powder tightly covered, and do not use it past the expiration date printed on the can.

## Nuts

New crops of nuts appear in super-markets from October to December, so autumn is a good time to buy a year's supply. I seal the nuts tightly in heavy-duty freezer bags or plastic freezer containers and freeze them for up to 1 year. It is easy to remove just what you need for a recipe. Defrost nuts before baking with them, so they do not turn batters cold and thick.

Toasting nuts improves their flavor. Taste a toasted nut, and you will see the difference. To toast nuts, spread them out in a single layer on a baking sheet and bake them in a preheated 325°F. oven. Shake the pan once or twice during baking to help them toast evenly. Bake walnuts and pecans for about 10 minutes, until fragrant; sliced or slivered almonds for 12 to 15 minutes, until they become golden; and blanched whole almonds and hazelnuts 15 to 20 minutes, until golden and fragrant. Just before the nuts are ready, you will smell a pleasant aroma of toasting nuts. Check them often at the end of baking to prevent burning.

Because hazelnuts must have their bitter peel removed before they are used, I recommend buying peeled hazelnuts. The King Arthur Flour Company (see Mail-Order Sources, page 117) ships them. To peel hazelnuts yourself, blanch untoasted hazelnuts for 5 minutes in boiling water, drain them in a strainer, and immerse them in cold water for about 5 minutes to cool. Drain them again and use a small sharp knife to peel them. The skin will slip off easily and the nuts are ready to toast. Any moisture will evaporate when the hazelnuts toast.

## Sugars and Sweeteners

Store all sugars in tightly covered containers to keep them dry and free from insects. Brown sugar must be kept airtight. Corn syrup and molasses should be stored in the refrigerator to prevent mold from forming. I use unsulphured molasses, which has not been processed with sulphur and has a milder flavor than sulphured molasses.

# mixing, baking, and storing tips

### Mixing

Maybe it is the chocolate chips that make any recipe seem easier, but many of these recipes can be mixed together in 15 minutes or less. Each recipe gives a mixing time, which assumes that your ingredients are already gathered and ready to go. If I wasn't sure whether something would take 15 or 20 minutes, I always chose the longer time, so many of the recipes might take even less time to mix than suggested.

Most of the batters in these cake recipes are mixed by one of two methods. Cake batter made with butter, such as the Chocolate–Chocolate Chip Layer Cake with Chocolate Frosting (page 100), is mixed by creaming softened butter and sugar and then beating in the eggs. The flour and liquid, if any, are added at the end in alternate additions. Thorough beating is important when creaming the butter and sugar and when adding the eggs, to develop the cake's structure. Adding the dry ingredients and the liquid is only a matter of blending them into the batter and does not require long beating. Chocolate chips and any nut or fruit additions are usually stirred in at the end.

For cakes that use oil as the shortening, such as the Orange Chocolate Chip Bundt Cake (page 103), the mixing is even easier. The light structure of the cake is developed through a thorough beating of the eggs with the sugar. Once this fluffy mixture is achieved, the mixing process is just a matter of incorporating the remaining ingredients to blend them into the batter.

Meringue cakes, angel food cakes, and chiffon cakes, as well as the fluffy Chocolate Marshmallow Frosting (page 94), depend on properly beaten egg whites for their light texture. The beaten egg whites should be shiny and form a soft point or peak when you dip a spoon into the egg whites and lift it out. At the soft peak stage, the moving beaters will form noticeable lines in the egg whites. These egg whites combine smoothly and easily with other mixtures.

To beat egg whites, start with the mixer on low speed. Add the cream of tartar, which helps stabilize the whites, and beat until it is dissolved. Increase the speed to medium and continue beating until soft peaks form. (It is easier to control the results on medium speed rather than on high speed.) Then begin to add any sugar. Sugar stabilizes the egg white foam, and once the sugar is added to egg whites, the mixture, or meringue, thickens. Add the sugar slowly so the egg whites have time to absorb it; adding 1 to 2 tablespoons of sugar every 15 to 30 seconds works well. Continue to beat until the whites form a stiff point or peak when you dip a spoon in the egg whites and lift it out.

When combining a lighter mixture with a heavier mixture or combining warm melted chocolate chips with cold whipped cream, you want to end up with a smooth result without deflating your carefully beaten or whipped mixture. The best method is to first use a whisk or rubber spatula to lighten the heavier mixture by stirring a small amount of the lighter mixture into it until smoothly combined. In the case of the melted chocolate and whipped cream, this gives a smooth chocolate base that is light enough to have the remaining whipped cream folded into it. This eliminates any hard bits of cooled chocolate forming as you fold the two mixtures together. Use the rubber spatula to fold the remaining light mixture into the heavier one.

Bring the edge of the spatula down to the bottom of the bowl and then bring the two mixtures up and over each other, turning the bowl as you fold, until they are smoothly blended.

## Baking

The baking question that I am asked most often is, "How do I know when something is done?" Since all ovens do not bake in exactly the same way, baking times are only a guide and are approximate. That is why my recipes include the word "about," as in "about 30 minutes." When the end of the baking time nears, begin checking with the visual tests. To be safe, begin checking about 3 to 5 minutes before the end of the suggested baking time for cookies, about 5 minutes before for bars, and about 8 to 10 minutes before for cakes or pies.

Each of those recipes gives at least one visual test. For example, a cookie recipe might call for browned edges or a pie or cheesecake recipe might say to give the pan a slight jiggle to see if the center is set. Cakes and bars are usually tested with a toothpick. Depending on the recipe, they are done when the toothpick comes out with a few moist crumbs clinging to it

or when it comes out clean. Touching the top of a cake to see if it feels firm and springs back is another such test, but this is then usually verified with the toothpick test. If you insert a toothpick into the edge of a cake and then insert it into the center, you will be able to feel the difference between a still-liquid center and a thoroughly baked edge. Resist any temptation to answer the telephone (voice of experience here), stay in the kitchen, and devote that time to enjoying your baking.

Leaving a baked cake in its pan for 10 to 15 minutes gives it time to settle and firm slightly. This more stable cake is then easily removed from the pan. Leaving baked cookies on their baking sheet for about 10 minutes gives them time to firm slightly. These firmer cookies will not break when they are removed from the baking sheet.

Finally, one doesn't always think about the temperature in the kitchen, but if you have ever watched ice cream melt quickly on the kitchen counter on a hot summer day or cream cheese take hours to soften in a cold kitchen, the effect it can have on mixing and baking becomes clear.

Batters or doughs may bake for a longer or shorter time depending on the temperature of the kitchen, since the mixture going into the oven may be at a colder or warmer temperature than usual. In a warm kitchen, chocolate melts fast and butter softens quickly; and cream should be whipped quickly, while it is still cold. In a cold kitchen, on the other hand, you may need to allow more time for butter and cream cheese to soften.

## Storing and Freezing

Generally, desserts that will be served at room temperatures are stored at room temperature, and ones that are served cold must be kept refrigerated. A chocolate-frosted cake or cheesecake stored in the refrigerator should sit at room temperature for 15 to 30 minutes before serving to soften the frosting or filling and bring out the flavors.

To protect soft frostings and whipped cream or soft cream toppings during storage, insert several toothpicks in the top of the dessert and cover it carefully with plastic wrap. The toothpicks keep the wrapping from squashing the topping, and the tiny holes will not be noticeable when the toothpicks are removed.

Cookies, bars, muffins, cakes without frosting, and cakes with rich chocolate or cream cheese frostings and fillings or chocolate glazes all freeze well for up to 1 month. The general guidelines are to cool anything thoroughly before wrapping it for the freezer, then wrap it carefully, enclosing it completely, and label it with the date and contents. Defrost it still wrapped so the condensation that forms during defrosting forms on the wrapper rather than on the baked good. I wrap cookies, bars, and muffins individually in plastic wrap, seal them in rigid freezer containers or tins, and freeze them. The containers protect them from breaking or crumbling, and the few minutes that it takes to wrap them individually keep them in prime condition. Cakes without frosting should be wrapped first in plastic wrap, then in heavy-duty aluminum foil. To freeze a frosted cake, first put it in the freezer unwrapped to firm the frosting or glaze, then wrap it in plastic wrap and heavy-duty foil.

Many of these desserts can be shipped off to friends and family.

Cookies, bars, muffins, and cakes without frosting make the best choices. They are good keepers and are less delicate than those with frostings.

The two secrets of good packaging are to use plenty of packing material and to double-box the dessert. Choose one or two rigid plastic containers or tins large enough to hold what you are mailing, then find a sturdy carton that will hold the containers and a generous amount of packing material. Arrange the wrapped items in the container, and fill any air spaces with crumpled wax paper. The container should be full but not tightly packed. Seal the container and then tape the top with masking tape to secure it. Wrap the container carefully in bubble wrap, newspaper, or other packing material, using enough to make a layer about an inch thick that provides a uniform cushion around the container. Put a cushion of crumpled newspaper or packing material in the bottom of the carton, add the container and cushion, and add enough packing material all around it so it fits securely in the carton. Seal the carton with sealing tape, and rest assured that you've

given your cookies a good send-off. Be sure to ship early in the week, Monday or Tuesday, so the box does not sit around in a shipping facility over the weekend.

# chocolate chip cookies and candies

I imagine that when Ruth Wakefield cut up a chocolate bar and added it to her Butter Drop Do Cookies more than seventy-five years ago, she had no idea that she was making a cookie that would sweep the country and become an American classic. Ruth owned the Toll House Inn in Wakefield, Massachusetts, and hers was the original Toll House Cookie. I have never tired of that cookie, but this chapter is an exploration of new frontiers for the chocolate chip cookie.

My explorations took me all over the cookie map. On the premise that more chocolate chips can only make a better cookie, I created a chocolate chip cookie that is so chock-full of chips it has four cups of chips mixed into two cups of dough. There are soft chocolate chip cookies and crisp chocolate chip wafer cookies. Chocolate chip cream makes a crunchy filling for buttery sandwich cookies. And two simple candies—a truffle and a bark—are made with melted chocolate chips.

# kitchen-sink chocolate chip cookies

There are chocolate chip cookies that have only chocolate chips and those that also include nuts, but these cookies have the whole shebang. There is just enough dough to hold the heaps, and I mean heaps, of chocolate chips, pecans, walnuts, and almonds together.

**mixing time** 10 minutes

**baking** 350° F. for about 14 minutes
   per batch

1 cup plus 2 tablespoons unbleached
   all-purpose flour

¾ teaspoon baking soda

½ teaspoon salt

½ cup (1 stick) unsalted butter,
   at room temperature

½ cup packed light brown sugar

6 tablespoons granulated sugar

1 large egg

1½ teaspoons vanilla extract

3 cups (18 ounces) semisweet
   chocolate chips

1 cup (4 ounces) pecan halves

1 cup (4 ounces) walnut halves
   or large pieces

1 cup (4 ounces) blanched whole
   almonds, toasted (see page 15)
   and chopped roughly in half

Position a rack in the middle of the oven. Preheat the oven to 350° F. Line 2 or 3 baking sheets with parchment paper.

Sift the flour, baking soda, and salt into a medium bowl and set aside.

In a large bowl, using an electric mixer on medium speed, beat the butter, brown sugar, and granulated sugar until smoothly blended, about 1 minute. Stop the mixer and scrape the sides of the bowl as needed during mixing. Add the egg and vanilla and mix until blended, about 1 minute. The mixture may look slightly curdled. On low speed, add the flour mixture, mixing just until it is incorporated. Mix in the chocolate chips, pecans, walnuts, and almonds until evenly distributed.

Use a tablespoon to drop well-rounded tablespoonfuls of dough (about 2 tablespoons each) onto the prepared baking sheets, spacing the cookies 2 inches apart.

Bake the cookies one sheet at a time until the edges are lightly browned and the centers are just slightly colored, about 14 minutes. Cool the cookies on the baking sheets for 10 minutes, then use a wide metal spatula to transfer the cookies to a wire rack to cool completely.

The cookies can be stored in a tightly covered container at room temperature for up to 4 days.

**Choices** You can add 1 cup of raisins, dried cranberries, or chopped dried apricots to the dough with the chips and nuts. White, bittersweet, or milk chocolate chips, or a combination, can be substituted for the semisweet chips.

# chock-full of chocolate chip cookies

One of my chocolate chip experiments was to see how many chocolate chips a cookie could comfortably hold. It turned out that two cups of dough plus four cups of chocolate chips makes cookies with at least fifty chocolate chips in every one. That's a chocolate blast of chips.

**mixing time** 10 minutes

**baking** 350° F. for about 15 minutes
 per batch

1¼ cups unbleached all-purpose flour

1 teaspoon baking soda

½ teaspoon salt

½ cup (1 stick) unsalted butter,
 at room temperature

½ cup packed light brown sugar

6 tablespoons granulated sugar

1 large egg

1 teaspoon vanilla extract

4 cups (24 ounces) semisweet
 chocolate chips

Position a rack in the middle of the oven. Preheat the oven to 350° F. Line 2 baking sheets with parchment paper.

Sift the flour, baking soda, and salt into a medium bowl and set aside.

In a large bowl, using an electric mixer on medium speed, beat the butter, brown sugar, and granulated sugar until smoothly blended, about 1 minute. Stop the mixer and scrape the sides of the bowl as needed during mixing. Add the egg and vanilla and mix until blended, about 1 minute. The mixture may look slightly curdled. On low speed, add the flour mixture, mixing just until it is incorporated. Mix in the chocolate chips until evenly distributed.

Use a tablespoon to drop heaping spoonfuls of dough (about 3 level tablespoons each) onto the prepared baking sheets, spacing the cookies 3 inches apart.

Bake the cookies one sheet at a time until the edges are lightly browned and the centers are golden, about

15 minutes. Cool the cookies on the baking sheets for 10 minutes. The cookies will flatten slightly as they cool. Use a wide metal spatula to transfer the cookies to a wire rack to cool completely.

The cookies can be stored in a tightly covered container at room temperature for up to 3 days.

**Choices** Bittersweet or milk chocolate chips can be substituted for the semisweet chips.

# banana-oatmeal chocolate chip cookies

Bananas add a new dimension to chocolate chip cookies. In addition to their flavor, the moist bananas produce a soft dough and, in turn, a soft cookie. These cookies are used in the Chocolate-Banana Whipped Cream Trifle (page 91). A plan-ahead idea is to wrap 16 of the cooled cookies well and freeze them to use at a later date for the trifle. For a double batch of cookies, double the ingredients.

**mixing time** 10 minutes

**baking** 350° F. for about 18 minutes per batch

1¼ cups unbleached all-purpose flour

1 teaspoon baking soda

¼ teaspoon salt

1 teaspoon ground cinnamon

6 tablespoons (¾ stick) unsalted butter, at room temperature

½ cup granulated sugar

½ cup packed light brown sugar

1 large egg

1 teaspoon vanilla extract

1 cup oatmeal (not quick-cooking)

2 cups (12 ounces) semisweet chocolate chips

2 bananas, cut into ¼- to ⅓-inch pieces

Position a rack in the middle of the oven. Preheat the oven to 350° F. Line 2 baking sheets with parchment paper and butter the paper.

In a small bowl, stir the flour, baking soda, salt, and cinnamon together; set aside.

In a large bowl, using an electric mixer on medium speed, beat the butter, granulated sugar, and brown sugar until smoothly blended, about 1 minute. Stop the mixer and scrape the sides of the bowl as needed during mixing. Add the egg and vanilla and mix until blended, about 1 minute. The mixture may look slightly curdled. On low speed, add the flour mixture, mixing just until it is incorporated. Mix in the oatmeal. Mix in the chocolate chips until evenly distributed. Use a large spoon to mix in the banana pieces, mixing just until they are evenly distributed and some of the pieces are mashed but most are still visible, about 20 seconds.

Use a tablespoon to drop heaping spoonfuls of dough (about 3 level tablespoons each) onto the prepared baking sheets, spacing the cookies 3 inches apart.

Bake the cookies one sheet at a time until the edges are lightly browned and the tops look dry, about 18 minutes. Cool the cookies on the baking sheets for 10 minutes, then use a wide metal spatula to transfer the cookies to a wire rack to cool completely.

The cookies can be stored in a tightly covered container, layered between sheets of wax paper, at room temperature for up to 3 days.

**Choices** Bittersweet or milk chocolate chips can be substituted for the semisweet chips.

# chocolate-chip-filled melting moments

It was on a summer afternoon in February while having lunch at the Bon Ton Café in Leura, Australia, that I spotted a display of butter-colored cream-filled sandwich cookies. They were called Melting Moments and are a specialty of Australia and New Zealand. As we traveled, we saw many variations of this deservedly popular cookie, but what remained constant in every one was the same delicate, soft, and melting quality that their name promises.

**mixing time** 10 minutes for cookies
and filling

**baking** 300° F. for about 30 minutes
per batch

### cookies

¹/₂ cup unbleached all-purpose flour

¹/₂ cup cake flour

³/₄ cup cornstarch

¹/₂ teaspoon baking powder

¹/₄ teaspoon salt

³/₄ cup (1¹/₂ sticks) unsalted butter,
at room temperature

³/₄ cup powdered sugar

1 teaspoon vanilla extract

### filling

¹/₄ cup (¹/₂ stick) unsalted butter,
at room temperature

³/₄ cup powdered sugar

1 teaspoon vanilla extract

¹/₄ cup miniature semisweet
chocolate chips

Position a rack in the middle of the oven. Preheat the oven to 300° F. Line 2 baking sheets with parchment paper.

**Make the cookies.** Sift both flours, the cornstarch, baking powder, and salt into a medium bowl and set aside.

In a large bowl, using an electric mixer on medium speed, beat the butter and powdered sugar until smooth and lightened slightly in color, about 1 minute. Stop the mixer and scrape the sides of the bowl as needed during mixing. Add the vanilla and mix until blended. On low speed, add the flour mixture, mixing just until it is incorporated and a smooth dough forms.

For each cookie, roll a level table-spoon of dough between the palms of your hands into a smooth ball. Place the cookies on the prepared baking sheets, spacing them 2 inches apart. Use a fork to gently flatten the cookies to 1¹/₄-inch disks, leaving an impression of the fork tines.

Bake the cookies one sheet at a time until the tops feel firm and the cookie bottoms are lightly browned, about 30 minutes; the tops of the cookies should not color. Cool the cookies on the baking sheets for 10 minutes, then use a wide metal spatula to transfer the cookies to a wire rack to cool completely.

**Make the filling.** In a medium bowl, use a wooden spoon to stir the butter, powdered sugar, and vanilla together until smooth. Stir in the chocolate chips.

Turn half of the cooled cookies bottom side up, and use a thin metal spatula to spread a rounded teaspoon of fill-ing evenly over each one. Place the remaining cookies right side up on the filling, and press gently.

The cookies can be stored in a tightly covered container at room tempera-ture for up to 5 days.

# chocolate-chocolate chip butter wafers

That A-team of baking—butter and chocolate—flavors these crisp-on-the-outside, chewy-on-the-inside cookies. The cookies are formed by rolling the dough into balls, then flattening them between the palms of your hands. Baking these cookies in a low oven prevents the bottoms from becoming too dark (read: burnt) before the insides of the cookie are done.

**mixing time** 5 minutes

**baking** 300° F. for about 16 minutes per batch

1½ cups unbleached all-purpose flour

⅓ cup unsweetened Dutch-process cocoa powder

¼ teaspoon salt

1 cup (2 sticks) unsalted butter, at room temperature

¾ cup plus 2 tablespoons sugar

2 large egg yolks

2 teaspoons vanilla extract

1 cup (6 ounces) miniature semisweet chocolate chips

Position a rack in the middle of the oven. Preheat the oven to 300° F. Line 2 baking sheets with parchment paper.

Sift the flour, cocoa powder, and salt into a medium bowl and set aside.

In a large bowl, using an electric mixer on medium speed, beat the butter and sugar until smooth and slightly lightened in color, about 1 minute. Stop the mixer and scrape the sides of the bowl as needed during mixing. Add the egg yolks and vanilla and mix until blended, about 1 minute. On low speed, add the flour mixture, mixing just until it is incorporated. Mix in the chocolate chips until evenly distributed.

Flour your hands lightly. For each cookie, use a tablespoon to scoop out a rounded spoonful of dough (about 2 level tablespoons), roll it between the palms of your hands into a smooth ball, and flatten between your palms to about a 2½-inch circle. Place the cookies on the prepared baking sheets, spacing them 2 inches apart. Flour your hands again if the dough becomes sticky during the rolling.

Bake the cookies one sheet at a time until the tops change from shiny to dull, about 16 minutes. The cookies will form a thin crusty top that feels firm if touched lightly. Cool the cookies on the baking sheets for 10 minutes, then use a wide metal spatula to transfer the cookies to a wire rack to cool completely.

The cookies can be stored in a tightly covered container at room temperature for up to 3 days.

# toffee chip snickerdoodles

Snickerdoodles are so popular because they have the same crisp edges and very chewy centers as a good chocolate chip cookie. The difference is that they are sweetened with white sugar only and they don't have any chocolate chips. These snickerdoodles correct that omission. They include chocolate chips and toffee chips and just might become the "new and improved" tradition.

**mixing time** 5 minutes

**baking** 350° F. for about 14 minutes per batch

2½ cups unbleached all-purpose flour

2 teaspoons cream of tartar

1 teaspoon baking soda

¼ teaspoon salt

2 cups sugar

1 teaspoon ground cinnamon

1 cup (2 sticks) unsalted butter, at room temperature

2 large eggs

1 teaspoon vanilla extract

¼ teaspoon almond extract

1 cup (6 ounces) semisweet chocolate chips

⅔ cup (about 4 ounces) chocolate toffee bits, such as Heath, or finely crushed chocolate-covered toffee

Position a rack in the middle of the oven. Preheat the oven to 350° F. Line 2 or 3 baking sheets with parchment paper.

Sift the flour, cream of tartar, baking soda, and salt into a medium bowl and set aside. In a small bowl, stir together ½ cup of the sugar and the cinnamon and set aside.

In a large bowl, using an electric mixer on medium speed, beat the butter and the remaining 1½ cups sugar until smoothly blended, about 1 minute. Stop the mixer and scrape the sides of the bowl as needed during mixing. Add the eggs, vanilla, and almond extract and mix until blended, about 1 minute. On low speed, add the flour mixture, mixing just until it is incorporated. Stir in the chocolate chips and toffee bits until evenly distributed. The dough will be soft.

For each cookie, use a tablespoon to scoop out a rounded spoonful of dough (about 2 level tablespoons), roll it between the palms of your hands into a smooth ball about 1½ inches in diameter, and then roll it in the cinnamon sugar mixture to coat evenly. Place the cookies 3 inches apart on the prepared baking sheets. (You will not use all of the cinnamon sugar, but working with a larger quantity makes coating the dough easier. Discard the leftover cinnamon sugar, since the dough has raw eggs in it.)

Bake the cookies one sheet at a time just until the edges are golden but the centers are still pale, about 14 minutes. If lightly touched, the center of the cookies should feel firm on the surface but soft underneath. The cookies puff up during baking and deflate to produce wrinkled tops (an indication of the good chewy center). Cool the cookies on the baking sheet for 5 minutes, then use a wide metal spatula to transfer them to a wire rack to cool thoroughly.

The cookies can be stored in a tightly covered container at room temperature for up to 3 days.

# chocolate chip truffles

Years ago, there was a popular cookbook called *The Elegant but Easy Cookbook.*
That same phrase describes truffles perfectly. Their preparation is easy, but the result
is totally elegant. Making truffles is as simple as heating cream and butter together
and stirring chocolate chips into the hot mixture to melt them. Add any flavorings
and chill the mixture to thicken it. That's it. Truffles can be arranged in decorative
tins for holiday gifts or served as a grand finale to a dinner party.

These dark and creamy truffles have a coating of miniature dark and white chocolate chips. L'Epicerie and King Arthur Flour (see Mail-Order Sources, page 117)
both sell miniature white chocolate chips. If miniature white chocolate chips are
unavailable, use all semisweet. Although the presentation is not as striking, the taste
is just fine.

**cooking time** 5 minutes

¾ cup heavy whipping cream

2 tablespoons unsalted butter,
  cut into 4 pieces

2 cups (11½ ounces) bittersweet
  chocolate chips

1 teaspoon vanilla extract

¾ cup miniature semisweet
  chocolate chips

¾ cup miniature white chocolate chips

**continued...**

In a medium saucepan, heat the cream and butter over low heat until the cream is hot and the butter melts. The mixture should form tiny bubbles and measure about 175° F. on a thermometer; do not let the mixture boil, or it may form a skin on top. (If this does happen, use a spoon to carefully lift off the skin and discard it.)

Remove the pan from the heat, add the bittersweet chocolate chips, and let them sit in the hot cream mixture for about 30 seconds to soften, then whisk until all of the chocolate is melted and the filling is smooth. Stir in the vanilla.

Pour the filling into a medium bowl and press a piece of plastic wrap directly against the surface. Poke a few small holes in the wrap with the tip of a knife to let steam escape. Refrigerate until the mixture is firm, about 3 hours, or overnight.

Set out 30 mini-muffin liners or candy papers. Lay a large piece of wax paper on the counter. Pour the miniature chocolate chips into a pie dish or shallow bowl. If the truffle mixture has been refrigerated overnight, it may need to sit at room temperature for about 30 minutes to soften enough to scoop easily. For each truffle, use a tablespoon to scoop out a level tablespoon of the truffle mixture, roll it quickly between the palms of your hands to form a ball about 1¼ inches in diameter, and place on the wax paper. Clean your hands when they become sticky with chocolate.
Roll each truffle ball in the chocolate chips to coat it thickly, pressing gently on the chips to help them adhere to the truffle, and place in a paper liner. Keep your hands clean so the white chips stay white (I learned this by experience).

The truffles can be stored in a tightly covered container in the refrigerator for up to 5 days. Let the truffles stand at room temperature for about 1 hour before serving. This ensures that they will be soft and creamy.

**Choices** Other flavoring ideas include almond extract, cinnamon, dissolved instant coffee granules, grated orange or lemon zest, fruit purees, rum, brandy, or liqueurs. Start with a small quantity of a flavoring, taste the mixture, and add more to your taste. You can make an assortment of flavors from one batch by dividing the warm chocolate mixture among several bowls and mixing a different flavor into each bowl.

# swiss fitness bark

For some mysterious reason, my husband's favorite candy bar can only be found in Switzerland. The bar has raisins, dried apricots, dried cherries, walnuts, and almonds held together by white chocolate. It is called a fitness bar, and I imagine the idea is that such a large quantity of fruit and nuts will make one more fit. Here is the American version, which can be put together in minutes and will save you a trip to Switzerland.

Using good-quality white chocolate chips (see page 10) is essential for smooth melting and good flavor.

**mixing time** about 8 minutes

1 cup (5¾ ounces) white chocolate chips, preferably Guittard

1 tablespoon canola or corn oil

2 tablespoons walnut halves or large pieces, toasted (page 15)

2 tablespoons unblanched whole almonds

¼ cup raisins

2 tablespoons chopped dried apricots

2 tablespoons dried cherries

Line a baking sheet with parchment paper.

Put the white chocolate chips and oil in a heatproof container or the top of a double boiler and place it over a saucepan of barely simmering water (or the bottom of the double boiler); the water should not touch the bowl. Stir until the white chocolate is melted and smooth.

Remove the container from the water and stir in the nuts and dried fruit. Pour the white chocolate mixture onto the lined baking sheet. Using a thin metal spatula, spread the mixture into a square about 7½ by 7½ inches. Let the bark sit until it is firm, about 1 hour.

Use a sharp knife to cut the bark into 12 pieces.

The bark can be refrigerated in a tightly covered tin for up to 1 week. Let sit at room temperature for about 15 minutes before serving.

# chocolate chip brownies, bars, muffins, and a tea loaf

Brownies and bars are the quick version of cookies. Instead of cookie dough, they call for a simple batter that is quickly spread into the pan and needs only to be cut into portions after baking. I decide on the size of bars by how I am going to use them, so many of these recipes give a range of the number of bars they will make. For a tea party or buffet dessert, cut smaller pieces that are easy to pick up and that allow guests to sample several varieties. For informal times such as picnics or snacks, larger pieces are more appropriate.

Once bars cool, they can be wrapped tightly and frozen. When freezing bars, I often cut them into large sections so I can decide on the size later. As with all frozen desserts, be sure to defrost bars with the wrapping on, so condensation forms on the wrapper, not the bars.

Line pans for bars and brownies with parchment paper or aluminum foil, letting the paper extend over two opposite ends of the pan. After the bars cool, loosen the edges of the bars and lift them out or turn them out of the pan. They will never stick to the pan, and chocolate chips will not get stuck to the bottom of the pan and be left behind. Once the bars are out of the pan, it is a cinch to cut them into even pieces. Another plus is the easy pan cleanup.

Muffins and quick breads also fall into the easy-to-mix-and-serve category. Think back to those high school home economics cooking classes: Muffins were first on the lesson plan. Chocolate Chip Zucchini Muffins (page 43) and the Orange, Cherry, and Chocolate Chip Tea Loaf (page 49) can comfortably go from morning coffee to brunch to afternoon tea to evening snack.

# chocolate chip fudge brownies with dark and white drizzle

Brown sugar and chocolate chips give a pure-fudge-all-the-way-through texture and taste to these brownies. Although the topping, with its swirls of melted dark and white chocolate chips, puts these brownies in the party class, they are quick and simple to mix.

**mixing time** 15 minutes for brownies and topping
**baking** 325° F. for about 45 minutes

**brownies**

1$\frac{2}{3}$ cups unbleached all-purpose flour
$\frac{1}{3}$ cup unsweetened Dutch-process cocoa powder, sifted
2 cups packed light brown sugar
1 teaspoon baking soda
$\frac{1}{4}$ teaspoon salt
$\frac{1}{2}$ cup (1 stick) unsalted butter, cut into pieces
1 large egg
1 teaspoon vanilla extract
1 cup sour cream
2 cups (12 ounces) semisweet chocolate chips

**topping**

$\frac{1}{3}$ cup semisweet chocolate chips
$\frac{1}{3}$ cup white chocolate chips
1 teaspoon vegetable oil

Position a rack in the middle of the oven. Preheat the oven to 325° F. Butter a 9-inch square baking pan and line the pan with a piece of parchment paper that is long enough to extend over two opposite sides of the pan. Butter the paper.

**Make the brownies.** In a large bowl, using an electric mixer on low speed, mix the flour, cocoa powder, brown sugar, baking soda, and salt to blend them. Add the butter pieces and continue mixing until the butter pieces are the size of peas, about 2 minutes. You will still see some loose flour. Stop the mixer and scrape the sides of the bowl as needed during mixing. Mix in the egg and vanilla. The batter will still look dry. Mix in the sour cream until the batter looks evenly moistened. You may see some lumps of butter. Mix in the chocolate chips.

Scrape the batter into the prepared pan. Bake just until the top feels firm and a toothpick inserted in the center comes out clean or with a few moist crumbs clinging to it, about 45 minutes. If the toothpick penetrates a chocolate chip, test another spot.

Transfer the pan to a wire rack to cool completely, about 1 hour. The brownies will sink in the center as they cool, because the center is especially moist.

**Make the topping.** Put the semisweet chocolate chips in a small heatproof bowl or the top of a double boiler and place over a saucepan of barely simmering water (or the bottom of the double boiler); the water should not touch the bowl. Stir until the chocolate is melted and smooth.

Use a fork to generously drizzle swirling lines of semisweet chocolate over the top of the uncut brownie.

Put the white chocolate chips and oil in a clean heatproof bowl or the clean top of the double boiler and place over the saucepan of barely simmering water (or the bottom of the double boiler); the water should not touch the bowl. Stir until the white chocolate is melted and smooth.

Use a fork to generously drizzle swirling lines of white chocolate over the top of the uncut brownie. Let it sit until the topping is firm, or refrigerate for about 15 minutes to firm the topping quickly.

Loosen the sides of the brownie from the unlined sides of the pan and use the ends of the paper to lift it from the pan. Use a large sharp knife to cut the brownie into 16 or 25 pieces and then a wide spatula to help slide the brownies off the paper.

The brownies can be covered and stored at room temperature for up to 3 days.

**Choices** Bittersweet or white chocolate chips can be substituted for the semisweet chips in the batter.

# brownies for a crowd

I have never met Betty Siewers, but I know her well through the good recipes that her son Joe has passed on to me. So when Joe sent me his mother's recipe for brownies, I knew I would be making a great brownie. They turned out to be thin, moist chocolate chip brownies made with chocolate syrup (so there is no chocolate to melt). The easy frosting is made with—what else?—chocolate chips. They bake in a rimmed baking sheet, also known as a jelly-roll pan, that produces about 35 brownies. So set up the picnic tables, make a date for the family reunion, or light up the barbecue; Betty's brownies can handle them all.

**mixing time** 15 minutes for brownies and frosting
**baking** 350° F. for about 20 minutes

1 cup unbleached all-purpose flour
$\frac{1}{2}$ teaspoon baking powder
$\frac{1}{4}$ teaspoon salt
$\frac{1}{2}$ cup (1 stick) unsalted butter, at room temperature
1 cup sugar
4 large eggs
1 teaspoon vanilla extract
1 $\frac{1}{2}$ cups chocolate syrup
$\frac{3}{4}$ cup (3 ounces) coarsely chopped walnuts
1 cup (6 ounces) semisweet chocolate chips

**frosting**

6 tablespoons ($\frac{3}{4}$ stick) unsalted butter
6 tablespoons whole milk
1 cup sugar
$\frac{1}{2}$ cup (about 3 ounces) bittersweet chocolate chips
1 teaspoon vanilla extract

Position a rack in the middle of the oven. Preheat the oven to 350° F. Butter a 15$\frac{1}{2}$-by-10$\frac{1}{2}$-by-1-inch baking pan (jelly-roll pan).

Sift the flour, baking powder, and salt into a medium bowl and set aside.

In a large bowl, using an electric mixer on medium speed, beat the butter and sugar until smoothly blended, about 1 minute. Stop the mixer and scrape the sides of the bowl as needed during mixing. Beat in 2 of the eggs until blended. Beat in the remaining 2 eggs and then the vanilla until blended, about 1 minute. The mixture may look slightly curdled. Mix in the chocolate syrup until smoothly blended. On low speed, add the flour mixture, mixing just until it is incorporated. Mix in the walnuts and chocolate chips.

Scrape the batter into the prepared pan, spreading it evenly. Bake just until the top feels firm when lightly touched and a toothpick inserted in the center comes out clean, about 20 minutes. If the toothpick penetrates a chocolate chip, test another spot.

Transfer the pan to a wire rack to cool completely, about 1 hour.

**Make the frosting.** In a medium saucepan, heat the butter, milk, and sugar over low heat, stirring often, until the sugar dissolves. Increase the heat to medium, bring the mixture to a boil, and boil for 30 seconds. Remove from the heat, add the chocolate chips, and let them sit in the hot milk mixture for about 30 seconds to soften. Add the vanilla and whisk until all of the chocolate chips are melted and the frosting is smooth.

Pour the frosting over the cooled brownies, using a thin metal spatula to spread it evenly. Let the brownies sit until the frosting is firm enough to cut neatly, about 30 minutes.

Use a small knife to loosen the brownies from the edges of the pan. Use a large sharp knife to cut the bars into 35 pieces (7 rows lengthwise and 5 rows across) and then a wide spatula to help lift the brownies from the pan.

The brownies can be carefully covered and stored at room temperature for up to 2 days. Store them in one layer to prevent the frosting from being squashed.

# butterscotch and fudge brownie bars

These brownies cover all the bases. Underneath a fudge brownie is a layer of chocolate chips, and underneath the chocolate chips is a layer of butterscotch walnut brownie. The different layers are made from one batter that is divided and flavored with melted butterscotch chips and melted chocolate chips. It's a home run for the brownies.

**mixing time** 10 minutes for brownies
and frosting
**baking** 350° F. for about 40 minutes

2½ cups (15 ounces) semisweet
chocolate chips
1 cup (6 ounces) butterscotch chips
2 cups unbleached all-purpose flour
1½ teaspoons baking powder
½ teaspoon salt
1 cup (2 sticks) unsalted butter,
at room temperature
1 cup packed light brown sugar
3 large eggs
2 teaspoons vanilla extract
¾ cup (3 ounces) coarsely
chopped walnuts

continued...

Position a rack in the middle of the oven. Preheat the oven to 350° F. Butter a 9-inch square baking pan and line the pan with a piece of parchment paper that is long enough to extend over two opposite sides of the pan. Butter the paper.

Put 1 cup of the chocolate chips in a heatproof bowl or the top of a double boiler and place it over a saucepan of barely simmering water (or the bottom of the double boiler); the water should not touch the bowl. Stir until the chocolate chips are melted and smooth. Set aside.

Put the butterscotch chips in another heatproof bowl or the (clean) top of the double boiler and place it over the saucepan of barely simmering water (or the bottom of the double boiler); the water should not touch the bowl. Stir until the butterscotch chips are melted and smooth. Set aside.

Sift the flour, baking powder, and salt into a medium bowl and set aside.

In a large bowl, using an electric mixer on medium speed, beat the butter and brown sugar until smoothly blended, about 1 minute. Stop the mixer and scrape the sides of the bowl as needed during mixing. Add the eggs and vanilla and mix until blended, about 1 minute. The mixture may look slightly curdled. On low speed, add the flour mixture, mixing just until it is incorporated.

Spoon 2 cups of the batter into a medium bowl. Use a large spoon to stir in the melted butterscotch chips until smoothly blended. Stir in the walnuts. Scrape the butterscotch batter into the prepared pan. Sprinkle the remaining 1½ cups chocolate chips over the butterscotch batter. Stir the melted chocolate chips into the remaining batter in the bowl until smoothly blended. Drop spoonfuls of the chocolate batter over the chocolate chips and then use a metal spatula to spread the chocolate batter evenly over the chocolate chips. Some chocolate chips may get mixed into the chocolate batter—this is fine.

Bake just until the top feels firm when lightly touched and a toothpick inserted in the center comes out clean or with a few moist crumbs clinging to it, about 40 minutes. If the toothpick penetrates a chocolate chip, test another spot. Transfer the pan to a wire rack to cool completely, about 1 hour.

Loosen the sides of the brownie from the unlined sides of the pan and use the ends of the paper to lift the brownies from the pan. Use a large sharp knife to cut the brownies into 16 or 25 pieces and then a wide spatula to help slide the brownies off the paper.

The brownies can be covered and stored at room temperature for up to 3 days.

# chocolate chip zucchini muffins

Nothing is certain but death, taxes, and the summer zucchini avalanche. These muffins are an ideal way to savor the bounty. For this muffin recipe I went to my friend Dianne Hannan, whose large garden has given her years of experience dealing with the zucchini harvest. Her recipe produces moist, nutty chocolate chip muffins.

A food processor or blender works well for finely chopping the zucchini. If it becomes partially pureed, that is fine.

**mixing time** 5 minutes

**baking** 350° F. for about 23 minutes

1¾ cups unbleached all-purpose flour

¾ teaspoon baking soda

½ teaspoon baking powder

1 teaspoon ground cinnamon

½ teaspoon salt

2 large eggs

1 cup sugar

½ cup corn or canola oil

1 teaspoon vanilla extract

1 cup finely chopped zucchini

¾ cup (3 ounces) coarsely
chopped walnuts

1 cup (6 ounces) semisweet
chocolate chips

Position a rack in the middle of the oven. Preheat the oven to 350° F. Line 12 muffin tin cups with paper liners. Spray the paper liners with nonstick spray.

In a medium bowl, stir the flour, baking soda, baking powder, cinnamon, and salt together. Set aside.

In a large bowl, whisk the eggs and sugar to blend them smoothly. Whisk in the oil and vanilla until blended. Use a large spoon to stir in the flour mixture just until incorporated. Stir in the zucchini, then stir in the walnuts and chocolate chips until evenly distributed.

Pour about ⅓ cup of batter into each paper liner. Bake until the tops are light brown and a toothpick inserted in the center of a muffin comes out clean, about 23 minutes. If the toothpick penetrates a chocolate chip, test another spot.

Cool the muffins in the pan on a wire rack for 5 minutes. Using pot holders to protect your hands, invert the muffin pan onto the rack and tap the bottom to release the muffins. Turn the muffins right side up to cool for about 15 minutes and serve warm, or let cool completely, about 45 minutes.

The muffins can be covered and stored at room temperature for up to 2 days.

**Choices** Bittersweet or milk chocolate chips can be substituted for the semisweet chips.

# coffee and white chocolate chip blondies

Sweet white chocolate and unsweetened coffee perfectly complement each other in these coffee-flavored blondies. Creating a decorative design of white chocolate over the top is as simple as letting white chocolate chips melt on top of the warm brownies and using the back of a spoon to swirl the melted chocolate.

**mixing time** 10 minutes

**baking** 350° F. for about 30 minutes

1⅓ cups unbleached all-purpose flour

1 teaspoon baking powder

½ teaspoon salt

½ cup (1 stick) unsalted butter, at room temperature

¾ cup packed light brown sugar

½ cup granulated sugar

2 large eggs

2 tablespoons instant coffee powder, dissolved in 2 tablespoons warm water

1 teaspoon vanilla extract

1 cup (5¾ ounces) plus 3 tablespoons white chocolate chips

Position a rack in the middle of the oven. Preheat the oven to 350° F. Butter a 9-inch square baking pan and line the pan with a piece of parchment paper that is long enough to extend over two opposite sides of the pan. Butter the paper.

In a small bowl, stir the flour, baking powder, and salt together. Set aside.

In a large bowl, using an electric mixer on medium speed, beat the butter, brown sugar, and granulated sugar until smoothly blended, about 1 minute. Stop the mixer and scrape the sides of the bowl as needed during mixing. Add the eggs, dissolved coffee, and vanilla and mix until blended, about 1 minute. The mixture may look slightly curdled. On low speed, add the flour mixture, mixing just until it is incorporated. Mix in 1 cup of the white chocolate chips until evenly distributed.

Scrape the batter into the prepared pan. Bake just until the top feels firm when lightly touched and a toothpick inserted in the center comes out clean, about 30 minutes.

Transfer the pan to a wire rack. Immediately sprinkle the remaining 3 tablespoons white chocolate chips over the top. Let the chips sit for 10 minutes, then use the back of a teaspoon to gently smear the melted chips to create large marbleized swirls of white chocolate. The swirls will not completely cover the bars. Cool until the topping is firm, about 1 hour. These are thin bars and may sink slightly in the center as they cool, because the center is especially moist.

Loosen the sides of the bars from the unlined sides of the pan and use the ends of the paper to lift the bars from the pan. Use a large sharp knife to cut the bars into 16 or 25 pieces and then a wide spatula to help slide the blondies off the paper.

The blondies can be covered and stored at room temperature for up to 3 days.

# chocolate chip cookie dough cheesecake bars

Some people think "cheesecake" is a synonym for dessert, and others feel the same way about chocolate chip cookies. These bars please both the cheesecake and the cookie crowd. They have a chocolate chip crumb crust, a chocolate chip cookie dough cheesecake filling, and melted chocolate chips swirled over the top.

**mixing time** 20 minutes for crust, dough, and filling

**baking** 325° F. for about 30 minutes for crust and filling

### crust

1½ cups graham cracker crumbs

5 tablespoons unsalted butter, melted

⅔ cup (4 ounces) miniature semisweet chocolate chips

### dough

5 tablespoons unsalted butter, at room temperature

⅓ cup packed light brown sugar

3 tablespoons granulated sugar

⅛ teaspoon salt

1 teaspoon vanilla extract

¾ cup unbleached all-purpose flour

1 cup (6 ounces) semisweet chocolate chips

### filling

10 ounces cream cheese, at room temperature

¼ cup sugar

1 large egg, at room temperature

1 teaspoon vanilla extract

⅓ cup semisweet chocolate chips

continued...

**Make the crust.** Position a rack in the middle of the oven. Heat the oven to 325° F. Butter a 9-inch square baking pan and line the pan with a piece of parchment paper that is long enough to extend over two opposite sides of the pan. Butter the paper.

In a medium bowl, stir the crumbs and melted butter together until the crumbs are evenly moistened. Stir in the chocolate chips.

Press the crumb mixture evenly over the bottom and 1 inch up the sides of the prepared pan. Bake for 6 minutes. Transfer the pan to a wire rack. Leave the oven on.

**Make the dough.** In a large bowl, using an electric mixer on medium speed, beat the butter, brown sugar, granulated sugar, salt, and vanilla until smoothly blended, about 1 minute. Decrease the speed to low and add the flour, mixing just to incorporate it. Stir in the chocolate chips. Set aside.

**Make the filling.** In a large bowl, using clean beaters, beat the cream cheese and sugar on low speed just until smooth. Mix in the egg and vanilla, beating just to blend them in.

Pour the cheesecake batter into the crust. Drop teaspoonfuls of the cookie dough over the top of the batter. Bake until the top feels dry and firm and looks set if given a gentle shake, about 30 minutes. Transfer the pan to a wire rack.

Put the 1/3 cup chocolate chips in a small heatproof bowl or the top of a double boiler and place it over a saucepan of barely simmering water (or the bottom of the double boiler); the water should not touch the bowl. Stir until the chocolate chips are melted and smooth.

Use a teaspoon to gently drizzle thin lines of melted chocolate over the top of the bars. Cool the bars completely in the pan, about 1 hour. The chocolate topping will be set when the bars are cool.

Loosen the sides of the bars from the unlined sides of the pan and use the ends of the paper to lift the bars from the pan. Use a large knife to cut the bars into 16 pieces, wiping the knife clean as needed (be careful to hold the knife blade away from you when wiping it), and slide the bars off the foil.

The bars can be covered and stored in the refrigerator for up to 3 days. Serve cold or at room temperature.

# orange, cherry, and chocolate chip tea loaf

Our friend Alan Roberts began to bake when he read my first cookbook. It has been years since he baked that first dessert, and he has become the chief baker for his large extended family. Now Alan sends me his baking discoveries, and I learn new recipes from him. They are always simple and have lots of fruit, like this quick bread made with dried cherries and fresh orange juice.

**mixing time** 10 minutes
**baking** 350° F. for about 65 minutes

2 cups unbleached all-purpose flour
1½ teaspoons baking powder
½ teaspoon baking soda
½ teaspoon salt
½ cup granulated sugar
½ cup packed light brown sugar
2 large eggs
2 tablespoons unsalted butter, melted
1 teaspoon vanilla extract
1 tablespoon grated orange zest
1 cup fresh orange juice
1 cup dried cherries
1 cup (6 ounces) semisweet chocolate chips
¾ cup (3 ounces) coarsely chopped pecans

Position a rack in the middle of the oven. Preheat the oven to 350° F. Butter a 9-by-5-by-3-inch loaf pan and line the bottom with a piece of parchment paper. Butter the paper.

Sift the flour, baking powder, baking soda, and salt into a large bowl. Stir in the granulated and brown sugars, pressing out any lumps in the brown sugar. Set aside.

In a medium bowl, using a fork, beat the eggs, melted butter, vanilla, and orange zest to combine them. Stir in the orange juice until blended. Make a well in the center of the flour mixture and use a large spoon to stir in the liquid mixture, mixing just to blend the ingredients into a smooth batter. Stir in the cherries, chocolate chips, and pecans.

Scrape the batter into the prepared pan. Bake until the top of the loaf is lightly browned and a toothpick inserted in the center comes out clean, about 1 hour and 5 minutes. There may be a few small cracks in the top of the loaf.

Let the loaf cool completely in the pan on a wire rack for about 1 hour.

Use a small sharp knife to loosen the loaf from the sides of the pan, and invert the loaf onto the wire rack. Carefully remove and discard the paper liner. Place a serving plate on the loaf and turn the loaf right side up. Use a large knife to cut the loaf into slices.

The loaf can be covered and stored at room temperature for up to 3 days.

# chocolate chip pies, tarts, and puddings

Pies and tarts are in the same dessert family, but pies are the homey, all-American branch, and tarts are the sophisticated branch. It is all in the eye of the beholder, though, because tarts are really no more difficult to make than pies. Since many puddings are essentially a pie or tart filling, they are also included here. And both the Layered Mocha Mousse (page 62) and the Chocolate Chip Bread Pudding (page 57) are "as easy as pie."

Making a good piecrust can be the bugaboo of even the most experienced baker, but these crusts are guaranteed to succeed. Two of the crusts are cookie crumb crusts, and the traditional piecrust is a cream cheese and butter dough that bakes into a buttery, tender crust every time. It may just become your first-choice crust for any pie. The two tart crusts are mixed as easily as a cookie dough—in fact, one of the crusts is a chocolate chip cookie dough.

# banana cream pie
# with graham cracker crunch

My husband, Jeff, pronounced this the deluxe version of banana cream pie. There is the classic vanilla pudding filling with plenty of bananas and whipped cream, but then the chocolate chips take over. The graham cracker crumb crust is heavily dotted with chocolate chips, and the whipped cream is covered with big pieces of the same crust mixture "glued" together with melted chocolate chips.

Graham cracker crumbs come in boxes and can be found in the baking section of supermarkets.

**mixing time** 20 minutes for crust, filling, and topping
**baking** 325° F. for 6 minutes

### crust and topping

2 1/4 cups graham cracker crumbs

2 tablespoons sugar

1/2 teaspoon ground cinnamon

1/2 cup (1 stick) unsalted butter, melted

1 cup (6 ounces) miniature semisweet chocolate chips

1/3 cup semisweet chocolate chips

### filling

1 1/2 cups whole milk

2 large eggs

1 large egg yolk

1/2 cup sugar

2 tablespoons unbleached all-purpose flour

1 teaspoon vanilla extract

### whipped cream topping

1 cup cold heavy whipping cream

1 tablespoon powdered sugar

1 teaspoon vanilla extract

3 bananas, sliced about 1/4 inch thick

continued...

**Make the crust and topping.** Position a rack in the middle of the oven. Preheat the oven to 325° F. Butter a 9-inch pie pan and a baking sheet.

In a large bowl, stir the graham cracker crumbs, sugar, and cinnamon together. Mix in the melted butter until the crumbs are evenly moistened. Mix in the miniature chocolate chips. Press 2¼ cups of the crust mixture evenly over the bottom and up the sides of the pie pan. Put the remaining crust mixture on the baking sheet and press it into a circle approximately 8 inches in diameter.

Bake the crust and topping for 6 minutes. Let cool to room temperature, about 45 minutes.

Put the ⅓ cup chocolate chips in a heatproof bowl or the top of a double boiler and place it over a saucepan of barely simmering water (or the bottom of the double boiler); the water should not touch the bowl. Stir until the chocolate chips are melted and smooth.

Use a small spoon to drizzle the melted chocolate over the topping on the baking sheet. Let the topping sit until the chocolate is firm.

**Make the filling.** In a medium saucepan, heat the milk over low heat just until it is hot; it should measure about

150° F. on an instant-read thermometer. Remove from the heat.

Meanwhile, in a medium bowl, whisk the eggs, egg yolk, and sugar until smooth. Whisk in the flour until smooth. Whisking constantly, slowly pour the hot milk into the yolk mixture. Pour the mixture back into the saucepan and cook over medium heat stirring constantly with a wooden spoon, making sure to reach into the corners to prevent scorching, until it thickens and just comes to a boil. Reduce the heat to low and cook at a gentle boil for about 1 minute, stirring constantly.

Pour the pastry cream through a fine strainer into a medium bowl. Stir in the vanilla. Press a piece of plastic wrap against the surface of the pastry cream and use the tip of a knife to poke a few holes in the plastic wrap to let steam escape. Refrigerate for 2 hours, or until cool to the touch. The pastry cream will thicken as it cools.

**Make the topping.** In a large bowl, using an electric mixer on medium-high speed, beat the cream, powdered sugar, and vanilla until firm peaks form.

Spread about one-third of the banana slices over the bottom of the crust. Gently stir the remaining banana slices into the cold filling, and spoon the

filling over the bananas. Use a thin metal spatula to spread the whipped cream over the filling. Use the edge of a wide metal spatula to cut the crunch into about 1-inch pieces, then use the spatula to lift the chunks of crunch and gently place them on the whipped cream, covering it thickly. Some plain pieces of chocolate may separate from the crumbs as you move them; this is fine. Sprinkle any crumbs over the top.

Serve, or cover carefully (see page 19) and refrigerate for as long as overnight. Serve cold.

# chocolate cream pie

Baking the chocolate chip graham cracker crust for a few minutes and melting chocolate chips for the filling is all the cooking required to making this chocolate pie topped with vanilla whipped cream. The soft topping, slightly firmer chocolate filling, and crisp crumb crust make a trio of contrasting textures.

Boxes of graham cracker crumbs can be found in the baking section of super-markets.

**mixing time** 15 minutes for crust, filling, and topping

**baking** 325° F. for 6 minutes

### crust

1 cup (about 3⅓ ounces) graham cracker crumbs

½ teaspoon ground cinnamon

5 tablespoons unsalted butter, melted

½ cup (3 ounces) miniature semisweet chocolate chips

### filling

1¾ cups heavy whipping cream

1½ cups (about 8½ ounces) bittersweet chocolate chips

1 teaspoon instant coffee powder, dissolved in 2 teaspoons hot water

6 tablespoons (¾ stick) unsalted butter, at room temperature

¾ cup powdered sugar

1 teaspoon vanilla extract

### topping

1 cup cold heavy whipping cream

2 tablespoons powdered sugar

1 teaspoon vanilla extract

**Make the crust.** Position a rack in the middle of the oven. Preheat the oven to 325° F. Butter a 9-inch pie pan.

In a medium bowl, stir together the graham cracker crumbs and cinnamon. Mix in the melted butter until the crumbs are evenly moistened. Mix in the chocolate chips.

Press the crust mixture evenly over the bottom and up the sides of the pie pan. Bake for 6 minutes.

Let the crust cool to room temperature, about 45 minutes.

**Make the filling.** In a medium saucepan, heat ¾ cup of the cream and the chocolate chips over low heat, stirring frequently, until the chocolate chips melt and the mixture is smooth. Stir in the dissolved coffee, remove from the heat, and set aside to cool until tepid.

In a large bowl, using an electric mixer on medium speed, beat the butter, powdered sugar, and vanilla until

smooth, about 1 minute. On low speed, beat in the chocolate mixture until blended. Cover and refrigerate for 10 minutes to cool and thicken slightly.

In a large clean bowl, using the electric mixer on medium-high speed, beat the remaining 1 cup cream until soft peaks form. Use a rubber spatula to fold the whipped cream into the cooled chocolate mixture. Using the spatula, spread the chocolate filling evenly in the cooled crust.

**Make the topping.** In a large bowl, using clean beaters, beat the cream, powdered sugar, and vanilla on medium-high speed until firm peaks form. Use a thin metal spatula to spread the whipped cream over the filling.

Cover the pie carefully (see page 19) and refrigerate for at least 2 hours to firm the filling further, or as long as overnight. Serve cold.

# pecan chocolate chip pie

My husband, Jeff, is not normally a pecan pie lover, but this pecan pie is the exception. Maybe it is the not-sweet-at-all cream cheese crust, maybe it is the addition of bittersweet chocolate chips, maybe it is that elusive taste of maple syrup in the filling, or maybe it is that this pie is just very good.

**mixing time** 20 minutes for crust and filling

**baking** 400° F. for 10 minutes, then 350° F. for about 28 minutes

### crust

1 cup unbleached all-purpose flour

1 tablespoon sugar

1/4 teaspoon salt

1/2 cup (1 stick) unsalted butter, at room temperature

3 ounces cold cream cheese, cut into 3 pieces

### filling

3 large eggs

1/2 cup granulated sugar

1/2 cup pure maple syrup

1/4 cup (1/2 stick) unsalted butter, melted

1/4 teaspoon salt

1 teaspoon vanilla extract

1 1/2 cups (6 ounces) coarsely chopped pecans

1 cup (5 3/4 ounces) bittersweet chocolate chips

Vanilla ice cream for serving (optional)

**Make the crust.** Sift the flour, sugar, and salt into a small bowl and set aside.

In a large bowl, using an electric mixer on low speed, beat the butter and cream cheese until smoothly blended, about 45 seconds. Mix in the flour mixture until the dough holds together and forms large clumps that come away from the sides of the bowl, about 30 seconds. (Or use a large spoon to stir the butter and cream cheese together until smoothly blended, then add the flour and continue stirring until clumps of smooth dough form.) Form the dough into a smooth ball, flatten it into a 6-inch disk, and wrap it in plastic wrap. Refrigerate for 30 minutes.

Butter a 9-inch pie pan. Lightly flour a work surface and rolling pin. Roll the dough into a 12-inch circle. Roll up the crust over the rolling pin and unroll it onto the pie pan. Fold 1/2 inch of the edge of the crust under itself to form a smooth edge. Use your thumb and forefinger to pinch the edge into a fluted border. Refrigerate the crust for 30 minutes.

Position a rack in the middle of the oven. Preheat the oven to 400° F.

**Make the filling.** In a large bowl, whisk the eggs to blend the whites and yolks, about 30 seconds. Add the sugar, maple syrup, melted butter, salt, and vanilla and whisk until smoothly blended, about 30 seconds. Stir in the pecans and chocolate chips. Pour the mixture into the chilled piecrust.

Bake the pie for 10 minutes at 400° F. Reduce the temperature to 350° F. and continue baking until the top of the pie looks firm and the filling seems set if you give the pan a gentle shake, about 28 minutes.

The pie can be served warm or at room temperature. While still warm, the pie has soft chocolate chips but crunchy pecans. Once the pie cools, the pecans and chocolate chips form a firm, chewy filling. Serve with vanilla ice cream, if desired.

The pie can be covered and stored at room temperature for up to 3 days.

# chocolate chip bread pudding

When my friend Becky Brace heard that I was writing a chocolate chip cookbook, her eyes lit up and she gave me the recipe for her favorite bread pudding. It is packed with miniature chocolate chips and dried apricots that become candied as they soak up the custard during baking.

A firm, close-grained egg bread, such as challah, is best for this pudding. The easiest way to cut up the dried apricots is to use scissors.

**mixing time** 10 minutes

**baking** 350° F. for about 40 minutes

8 cups 1-inch bread cubes with crust (about six ½-inch-thick slices)

¾ cup dried apricots, cut into ½-inch pieces

⅔ cup (4 ounces) miniature semisweet chocolate chips

½ cup (1 stick) unsalted butter, cut into pieces

½ cup sugar

2 cups whole milk

¼ cup dark rum

2 large egg yolks

1 cup cold heavy whipping cream (optional)

Position a rack in the middle of the oven. Preheat the oven to 350° F. Butter a 9-by-13-by-2-inch baking dish or pan.

Put the bread cubes in the baking dish and bake for 5 minutes to toast the bread slightly, stirring once. Sprinkle the apricots and chocolate chips over the bread and set aside.

In a medium saucepan, heat the butter, sugar, and milk over low heat, stirring frequently, until the butter melts and the sugar dissolves. Pour the mixture into a large bowl, stir in the rum, and set aside for 5 minutes to cool slightly.

Whisking constantly, add the egg yolks to the warm milk mixture. Pour this custard over the bread mixture in the baking dish. Use a large spoon to press the apricots into the mixture if they float to the top.

Bake until the top is lightly browned and crusty, the custard is absorbed, and the pudding seems set if you give it a slight jiggle, about 40 minutes. Let the pudding sit for about 10 minutes, and serve it warm.

Pass a pitcher of fresh cream to pour over the pudding, if desired.

**Choices** Dried cherries, cranberries, or raisins can be substituted for the apricots or added to them.

**Note** A 13-by-9-inch pan makes a thin bread pudding. For a thick, soft version, bake the pudding in a 9-inch square baking pan or a casserole with about the same dimensions. Baking time will be about 55 minutes.

# chocolate chip cookie and cream tart

This tart is a combination of three classics: chocolate chip cookies, whipped cream, and fudge sauce. The crust is a thick chocolate chip cookie that is spread with chocolate truffle fudge sauce and covered with vanilla whipped cream. As it cools, the center of the baked cookie sinks slightly, which makes room for the truffle filling.

**mixing time** 20 minutes for crust, filling, and topping

**baking** 350° F. for about 17 minutes

### crust

1 cup plus 2 tablespoons unbleached all-purpose flour

1/2 teaspoon baking soda

1/2 teaspoon salt

1/2 cup (1 stick) unsalted butter, melted and cooled slightly

1/2 cup packed light brown sugar

6 tablespoons granulated sugar

1 large egg

1 teaspoon vanilla extract

1 cup (6 ounces) semisweet chocolate chips

### filling

1/4 cup heavy whipping cream

1 tablespoon unsalted butter

2/3 cup (4 ounces) semisweet chocolate chips

1/2 teaspoon vanilla extract

### topping

1 cup cold heavy whipping cream

1 tablespoon powdered sugar

1 teaspoon vanilla extract

**Make the crust.** Preheat the oven to 350° F. Butter a 10-inch springform pan.

Sift the flour, baking soda, and salt into a medium bowl and set aside.

In a large bowl, using an electric mixer on medium speed, beat the butter, brown sugar, and granulated sugar until smoothly blended, about 1 minute. Add the egg and vanilla and mix until blended, about 1 minute. The mixture may look slightly curdled. On low speed, add the flour mixture, mixing just until it is incorporated. Mix in the chocolate chips.

Use your fingers to spread the dough evenly over the bottom of the prepared pan. Bake just until the top begins to turn golden but the center is still soft, about 17 minutes. Cool the crust in the pan on a wire rack.

**Make the filling.** In a medium saucepan, heat the cream and butter over low heat until the cream is hot and the butter melts. The mixture should form tiny bubbles and measure about 175° F. on an instant-read thermometer; do not let the mixture boil. Remove the pan from the heat, add the choco-late chips, and let them sit in the hot cream mixture for about 30 seconds to soften, then whisk until all of the chocolate is melted and the filling is smooth. Stir in the vanilla. Let the filling cool and thicken at room temperature for about 30 minutes.

Leaving a 1-inch edge uncovered, spread the sauce over the crust. Refrigerate for about 30 minutes to firm the filling.

Use a small sharp knife to loosen the sides of the crust from the pan and then remove the sides of the pan. Use a sharp knife to loosen the crust from the bottom of the pan and then a wide metal spatula to slide the tart onto a platter.

**Make the topping.** In a large bowl, using an electric mixer on medium-high speed, beat the cream, powdered sugar, and vanilla until firm peaks form. Spread the whipped cream over the chocolate filling, mounding it slightly in the center.

Serve, or cover carefully (see page 19) and refrigerate for as long as overnight. Serve cold.

# hazelnut and chocolate chip tart

Stroll into any chocolate shop in Italy, and you will find trays of chocolates rolled in hazelnuts. Pass by the *pasticceria* and you will see chocolate and hazelnut cakes. Step into a gelateria, and you will discover hazelnut and chocolate (*gianduja*) gelato. I have savored all of them. Italians have long realized the greatness of the chocolate-and-hazelnut combination. Here a buttery hazelnut crust is filled with bittersweet chocolate chips (instant filling) that melt together under a hazelnut lattice crust.

**mixing time** 10 minutes
**baking** 350° F. for about 35 minutes

1¼ cups (5 ounces) peeled toasted hazelnuts (see page 15)

1¾ cups unbleached all-purpose flour

¾ cup sugar

½ teaspoon baking powder

2 teaspoons ground cinnamon

1 cup (2 sticks) cold unsalted butter, cut into approximately ½-inch pieces

3 large egg yolks

2 teaspoons vanilla extract

2 cups (11½ ounces) bittersweet chocolate chips

Preheat the oven to 350° F. Butter a 9-inch springform pan.

In a food processor fitted with the steel blade, process the hazelnuts until finely ground, about 1 minute.

In a large bowl, using an electric mixer on low speed, mix the hazelnuts, flour, sugar, baking powder, and cinnamon just to blend them. Add the butter pieces and mix until the butter pieces are the size of peas, about 2 minutes. You will still see loose flour. Mix in the egg yolks and vanilla until large crumbs that cling together form and the dough pulls away from the sides of the bowl, about 30 seconds.

Remove 2 cups of the dough to use for the lattice topping. Wrap it in plastic wrap and refrigerate it. Transfer the remaining dough to the prepared pan and press it evenly over the bottom and 1¼ inches up the sides. Sprinkle the chocolate chips evenly over the crust.

Remove the reserved dough from the refrigerator. Use a generous 3 tablespoons of dough for the longest ropes and less for the shorter ropes; if a rope breaks, just pinch it back together. Roll a piece of dough back and forth to form a 9-inch-long rope about ½ inch in diameter. Place this rope across the middle of the tart. Roll two 8-inch ropes, and, spacing them about 2 inches apart, place one on either side of the center rope. Roll two 4½- inch ropes, and place them near the sides of the tart. Give the pan a half turn, and repeat the rope rolling, placing 5 more ropes over the first ropes to make a crosshatch pattern.

Bake the tart until the top is golden brown, about 35 minutes. Cool the tart in the pan on a wire rack for about 1 hour for a soft chocolate filling, or 2 hours for a firm filling.

Use a small sharp knife to loosen the sides of the crust from the pan, and then remove the sides of the pan. Use a sharp knife to loosen the tart from the bottom of the pan and then a wide metal spatula to slide the tart onto a platter.

The tart can be covered and stored at room temperature for up to 2 days.

**Choices** Semisweet, milk chocolate, or a mixture of chips can be substituted for the bittersweet chips.

# layered mocha mousse

Get out your prettiest party glasses to fill with layers of coffee whipped cream and chocolate mocha mousse for this make-ahead dessert. Be sure to spread the layers neatly to the edges of each glass so the different colors show through.

The truffle sauce must cool but still remain pourable before it is used. Warm truffle sauce would cause the whipped cream to deflate when the two are mixed.

**mixing time** 10 minutes
**cooking time** 5 minutes

6 tablespoons cold heavy whipping cream, plus 2 cups
1 tablespoon unsalted butter
1 cup (5¾ ounces) bittersweet chocolate chips
1½ teaspoons vanilla extract
⅓ cup powdered sugar
2½ teaspoons instant coffee powder

In a medium saucepan, heat the 6 tablespoons cream and the butter over low heat until the cream is hot and the butter melts. The mixture should form tiny bubbles and measure about 175° F. on a thermometer; do not let the mixture boil, or it may form a skin on top. (If this does happen, use a spoon to carefully lift off the skin and discard it.) Remove the pan from the heat, add the chocolate chips, and let them sit in the hot cream mixture for about 30 seconds to soften, then whisk until all of the chocolate is melted and the filling is smooth. Stir in ½ teaspoon of the vanilla.

Transfer ¾ cup of the truffle sauce to a large bowl and leave the remaining sauce in the pan, for topping the mousse. Set aside to cool to room temperature, about 30 minutes.

Have ready 6 stemmed glasses or goblets with at least a 10-ounce capacity.

In a large bowl, using an electric mixer on medium-high speed, beat the remaining 2 cups cold cream, the pow-

dered sugar, instant coffee, and the remaining 1 teaspoon vanilla until firm peaks form. (The coffee will dissolve as the cream whips.) Transfer 1½ cups of the whipped cream to a small bowl and set aside. Whisk about 1 cup of the remaining whipped cream into the cooled truffle sauce in the large bowl, then fold the remaining whipped cream into the mousse.

Spoon about 2 tablespoons of mousse into the bottom of each glass. Spoon about 2 tablespoons of the reserved coffee whipped cream over the mousse, spreading it to the edges of the glass. Repeat the layering with the mousse and coffee whipped cream. Use a small spoon to drizzle the reserved chocolate sauce over the top of each glass. (Warm the sauce briefly over low heat if necessary to make it pourable.)

Cover the mousse and refrigerate until cold and set, about 2 hours, or as long as overnight. Serve cold.

**Choices** Two tablespoons of rum can be whipped with the cream.

## chocolate chip cakes without frosting

These cakes travel the cakewalk from an informal loaf to a tall, impressive tube cake to crumb cake squares to individual ramekins of warm chocolate chip cake. They do have several things in common. Each one is simple to mix and can be put together quickly. Any toppings or fillings bake right with the cakes. And with the exception of an occasional dusting of powdered sugar or the addition of a scoop of ice cream, the cakes are ready to serve as soon as they cool.

Tea party, picnic, dinner party, or garden party—you name it, there is a cake here for any time of day or night. It could be the Raspberry Chocolate Chip Crumbs Cake (page 66) to take along to picnics and barbecues, the Chocolate Chip–Crumb Pound Cake (page 73) to serve for tea, or the Strawberry and White Chocolate Chip Cheesecake (page 76) for serving at a party. The Lemon and Chocolate Chip Loaf Cake (page 69) is just right for packing and sending off for gifts.

Three of these cakes bake in a tube pan that has a fixed bottom. This ensures that the batter will not leak out of the pan. You can find these pans in cookware stores and even in some supermarkets. However, when my friend Louise Shames tested the In-the-Chips Marble Cake (page 79), she had to use a tube pan with a removable bottom, and she didn't have a problem. To be safe, she did wrap the pan in aluminum foil, but it didn't leak.

# raspberry and chocolate chip crumbs cake

The plural of the word "crumb" in this title is not a typo. The yellow cake holds the raspberries, and the topping is made up of buttery crumbs that are loaded with tiny chocolate chips.

Defrost frozen raspberries in the refrigerator to keep them in the best condition. If the raspberries are cold or still partially frozen when they are mixed into the cake batter, the cake will need to bake for about 5 minutes more.

**mixing time** 15 minutes for topping
and cake

**baking** 350° F. for about 50 minutes

**topping**

1 cup unbleached all-purpose flour

3/4 cup packed light brown sugar

1/4 teaspoon salt

1/2 cup (1 stick) cold unsalted butter, cut
into 1/2-inch pieces

1 cup (6 ounces) miniature semisweet
chocolate chips

**cake**

1 3/4 cups unbleached all-purpose
flour

1 1/2 teaspoons baking powder

1/4 teaspoon salt

4 ounces (1 stick) unsalted butter,
at room temperature

3/4 cup sugar

2 large eggs

1 teaspoon vanilla extract

1 teaspoon almond extract

1/2 cup whole milk

3 cups fresh raspberries or one
12-ounce bag unsweetened frozen
raspberries, defrosted

Powdered sugar for dusting

Position a rack in the middle of the oven. Preheat the oven to 350° F. Butter a 9-inch square baking pan and line the pan with a piece of parchment paper that is long enough to extend over two opposite sides of the pan. Butter the paper.

**Make the topping.** In a large bowl, stir the flour, brown sugar, and salt together, breaking up any lumps of brown sugar. Add the butter pieces. Use the paddle attachment of an electric mixer on low speed, a pastry blender, or your fingertips to mix the ingredients together until crumbs form. The largest crumbs should be about 1/2 inch in size. Stir in the chocolate chips. Set aside.

**Make the cake.** Sift the flour, baking powder, and salt into a medium bowl. Set aside.

In a large bowl, using an electric mixer on medium speed, beat the butter and sugar until smoothly blended, about 1 minute. Stop the mixer and scrape the sides of the bowl as needed during mixing. Add the eggs, vanilla, and almond extract and mix until smoothly blended, about 1 minute. The mixture may look slightly curdled. On low

speed, add half of the flour mixture, mixing just until it is incorporated. Mix in the milk just until blended. Add the remaining flour mixture, mixing just until it is incorporated. Sprinkle the raspberries over the batter and gently fold them in, folding just enough to distribute them fairly evenly. Raspberries are delicate and should be mixed as little as possible.

Scrape the batter into the prepared pan. Sprinkle the reserved crumb mixture over the top of the batter. Bake until the top is lightly browned and a toothpick inserted in the center comes out clean, about 50 minutes.

Cool the cake in the pan on a wire rack until the chocolate chips are firm, about 1½ hours. To speed this, you can cool the cake for 30 minutes on the rack, then refrigerate it for about 15 minutes.

Use a small sharp knife to loosen the cake from the sides of the pan, and invert the cake onto the wire rack. Carefully remove and discard the paper liner. Place a serving plate on the cake and turn the cake right side up. To serve, dust the top lightly with powdered sugar and cut into 12 squares.

The cake can be covered and stored at room temperature for up to 3 days.

**Choices** White chocolate or bittersweet chocolate chips can be substituted for the semisweet chocolate chips in the crumb topping.

# rhubarb and white chocolate chip buckle

Maine may be at the end of the line for the arrival of spring, but when those first red stalks of rhubarb appear in markets or pop up in the garden, we know it is time to shed our winter mantle of cozy desserts. That is when I make this combination of tart rhubarb and sweet white chocolate chips.

Rhubarb leaves are toxic. Be sure to remove any that remain on the stalks and discard them.

**mixing time** 10 minutes
**baking** 350° F. for about 50 minutes

### topping

1 cup unbleached all-purpose flour
1 cup packed light brown sugar
1/2 teaspoon ground cinnamon
5 tablespoons unsalted butter, melted

### cake

2 cups unbleached all-purpose flour
1 1/2 teaspoons baking powder
1 teaspoon ground cinnamon
1/2 teaspoon salt
6 tablespoons (3/4 stick) unsalted butter, at room temperature
2/3 cup sugar
1 teaspoon finely grated orange zest
1 large egg
1 teaspoon vanilla extract
1/2 cup whole milk
3 cups coarsely chopped rhubarb
1/2- to 3/4-inch cubes (about 12 ounces)
1 1/2 cups (about 9 ounces) white chocolate chips

Powdered sugar for dusting

Position a rack in the middle of the oven. Preheat the oven to 350° F. Butter a 9-inch square baking pan and line the pan with a piece of parchment paper that is long enough to extend over two opposite sides of the pan. Butter the paper.

**Make the topping.** In a medium bowl, stir the flour, brown sugar, and cinnamon until blended, breaking up any lumps of sugar. Stir in the melted butter until the mixture is evenly moistened and crumbly. Set aside.

**Make the cake.** Sift the flour, baking powder, cinnamon, and salt into a medium bowl. Set aside.

In a large bowl, using an electric mixer on medium speed, beat the butter, sugar, and orange zest until smoothly blended, about 1 minute. Stop the mixer and scrape the sides of the bowl as needed during mixing. Add the egg and vanilla and mix until blended, about 1 minute. The mixture may look slightly curdled. On low speed, add half of the flour mixture, mixing just until it is incorporated. Mix in the milk to blend it. Mix in the remaining flour mixture until it is incorporated and the batter looks smooth. Mix in the rhubarb and white chocolate chips until evenly distributed.

Scrape the batter into the prepared pan. Bake until the top is lightly browned and a toothpick inserted in the center comes out clean, about 50 minutes.

Cool the cake completely in the pan on wire rack, about 1 hour.

Use a small sharp knife to loosen the cake from the sides of the pan, then invert the cake onto the wire rack. Carefully remove and discard the paper liner. Place a serving plate on the cake and turn the cake right side up. Dust the top lightly with powdered sugar before serving, and cut into 12 squares.

The cake can be covered and stored at room temperature for up to 3 days.

# lemon and chocolate chip loaf cake

Chocolate and lemon is a sleeper combination, and this chocolate chip cake drenched with fresh lemon syrup makes a good introduction. Once you try it, you will be hooked.

Lemon zest, the yellow part of the peel without any of the bitter white pith, adds an intense lemony flavor to the cake.

**mixing time** 10 minutes

**baking** 350° F. for about 50 minutes

### cake

1½ cups unbleached all-purpose flour

1 teaspoon baking powder

¼ teaspoon salt

½ cup (1 stick) unsalted butter,
  at room temperature

1 cup sugar

2 teaspoons finely grated lemon zest

2 large eggs

1 teaspoon vanilla extract

½ teaspoon almond extract

½ cup whole milk

1 cup (6 ounces) miniature semisweet
  chocolate chips

### lemon syrup

⅓ cup sugar

3 tablespoons fresh lemon juice

Position a rack in the middle of the oven. Preheat the oven to 350° F. Butter a 9-by-5-by-3-inch loaf pan and line the bottom with a piece of parchment paper. Butter the paper.

**Make the cake.** Sift the flour, baking powder, and salt into a medium bowl. Set aside.

In a large bowl, using an electric mixer on medium speed, beat the butter, sugar, and lemon zest until smoothly blended, about 1 minute. Stop the mixer and scrape the sides of the bowl as needed during mixing. Add the eggs, vanilla, and almond extract and mix until blended, about 1 minute. The mixture may look slightly curdled. On low speed, add half of the flour mixture, mixing just until it is incorporated. Mix in the milk just until blended. Add the remaining flour mixture, mixing just until it is incorporated. Mix in the chocolate chips.

Scrape the batter into the prepared pan. Bake until the top is lightly browned and a toothpick inserted in the center comes out clean, about 50 minutes.

**Make the lemon syrup.** In a small saucepan, about 10 minutes before the cake is done, heat the sugar and lemon juice over medium heat, stirring constantly, until the sugar dissolves. Do not boil. Set aside.

As soon as the cake comes out of the oven, use a toothpick to poke holes all over the top. Pour the warm syrup evenly over the top of the cake, using all of it. Let the cake cool completely in the pan on a wire rack, about 1 hour.

Use a small sharp knife to loosen the cake from the sides of the pan, and invert the cake onto the wire rack. Carefully remove and discard the paper liner. Place a serving plate on the cake and turn the cake right side up. Use a large knife to cut the cake into slices.

The cake can be covered and stored at room temperature for up to 3 days.

# cinnamon and chips chiffon cake

Chiffon cakes combine the best of two cake worlds. They have the qualities of a light angel food cake and a moist, oil-enriched sponge cake all in one. Chiffon cake bakes in an ungreased tube pan and one that does not have a nonstick finish. Unlike most cakes, the cake should stick to the pan. The batter climbs slowly up the sides of the pan as it bakes, and then the cake clings to the pan as it cools, maintaining its high, light structure.

**mixing time** 10 minutes
**baking** 325° F for about 1 hour

2 cups cake flour
1⅓ cups sugar
1 teaspoon baking powder
½ teaspoon salt
4 teaspoons ground cinnamon
½ cup canola or corn oil
6 large eggs, separated
⅔ cup water
2 teaspoons vanilla extract
1½ cups (9 ounces) miniature
  semisweet chocolate chips
½ teaspoon cream of tartar

**garnish**
1 tablespoon powdered sugar
⅛ teaspoon ground cinnamon
¼ teaspoon unsweetened cocoa
  powder

**continued...**

Preheat the oven to 325° F. Have ready a 9½- or 10-inch fixed-bottom tube pan with at least 3¾-inch-high sides. Do not use a nonstick pan.

Sift the cake flour, 1 cup of the sugar, the baking powder, salt, and cinnamon into a large bowl. Use a large spoon to make a well in the center of the flour mixture and add the oil, egg yolks, water, and vanilla. Using an electric mixer on medium speed, beat the mixture until it is smooth and thick, about 3 minutes. Stop the mixer and scrape the sides of the bowl as needed during mixing. Use a rubber spatula to fold in the chocolate chips. Set aside.

In another large bowl, with clean beaters, beat the egg whites and cream of tartar on low speed until the whites are foamy and the cream of tartar dissolves. Beat on medium speed until the egg whites look shiny and smooth and the movement of the beaters forms lines in the beaten whites. If you stop the mixer and lift up the beaters, the whites should cling to the beaters. Slowly beat in the remaining ⅓ cup of sugar, 1 tablespoon at a time, then beat for about 1 minute to firm, glossy peaks. Stir about one-third of the beaten egg whites into the egg yolk mixture, then fold in the remaining egg whites until no white streaks remain.

Scrape the batter into the tube pan and gently smooth the top. Bake until the top of the cake feels firm when you gently press it and any small cracks in the top look dry, about 1 hour.

Invert the pan onto a narrow-necked bottle (a full wine bottle is stable and works well) and let cool for 1 hour.

Remove the pan from the bottle and run a thin knife around the sides and center tube of the pan to loosen the cake. Remove the cake from the pan by inverting it onto a flat serving plate, then place a wire rack on the bottom of the cake and invert the cake onto the rack, so the cake is right side up. Cool the cake thoroughly on the wire rack.

Mix the powdered sugar and cinnamon together, put the mixture in a small strainer, and dust it evenly over the top of the cake. Dust the powdered sugar mixture lightly with the cocoa powder. Slip a large metal spatula under the cake and slide it onto a serving plate. (Once cooled, the cake is sturdy and easy to move.) Use a serrated knife to cut the cake into slices.

The cake can be covered and stored at room temperature for up to 3 days.

# chocolate chip-crumb pound cake

Small changes can make a big difference in baking. I took the pound cake recipe that I have been making for many years (and it is a very good pound cake), substituted cream cheese for one stick of the butter, reduced the flour by about 25 percent, and omitted the liquid. The result was this extremely moist and super-tender pound cake. Then came the bigger change of streaking it with a chocolate-chip-crumb mixture and sprinkling the top with more of the same. A very good cake became great—and the best pound cake that I have ever made.

**mixing time** 15 minutes for topping and cake

**baking** 325° F. for about 1 hour and 35 minutes

### topping

1 cup unbleached all-purpose flour

6 tablespoons light brown sugar

$1/4$ cup granulated sugar

$1/2$ teaspoon ground cinnamon

$1/4$ cup ($1/2$ stick) unsalted butter, melted

1 cup (6 ounces) miniature semisweet chocolate chips

### cake

3 cups unbleached all-purpose flour

1 teaspoon baking powder

$1/8$ teaspoon salt

$1^1/2$ cups (3 sticks) unsalted butter at room temperature

8 ounces cream cheese, at room temperature

$2^3/4$ cups sugar

6 large eggs, at room temperature for 1 hour

2 teaspoons vanilla extract

$1/2$ teaspoon almond extract

Powdered sugar for dusting

**continued...**

Preheat the oven to 325° F. Butter the bottom, sides, and center tube of a 9½- or 10-inch fixed-bottom tube pan with at least 3¾-inch-high sides. Line the bottom of the pan with a ring of parchment paper and butter the paper.

**Make the topping.** In a medium bowl, stir the flour, brown sugar, granulated sugar, and cinnamon until blended. Stir in the melted butter until the mixture is evenly moistened and crumbly. Stir in the chocolate chips. Set aside.

**Make the cake.** Sift the flour, baking powder, and salt into a medium bowl and set aside.

In a large bowl, using an electric mixer on medium speed, beat the butter and cream cheese until blended. Add the sugar and beat until fluffy and lightened to a creamy color, about 3 minutes. Stop the mixer and scrape the sides of the bowl as needed during mixing. Put the eggs in a small bowl and use a fork to beat them lightly. Add the eggs in 3 additions, mixing for about 1 minute after each addition until blended into the batter. Add the vanilla and almond extract and beat for 1 minute. On low speed, add the flour mixture, mixing just until it is incorporated.

Pour half of the batter into the prepared pan. Sprinkle 1½ cups of the crumb mixture over the batter. Pour the remaining batter over the crumbs and use a thin metal spatula to spread the batter evenly. Sprinkle the remaining crumbs evenly over the top, pressing them gently into the batter. Bake until the top looks light brown under the crumbs (some of the plain top will show through) and a toothpick inserted in the center comes out clean, about 1 hour and 35 minutes.

Let the cake cool in the pan on a wire rack until the chocolate chips on top are firm, about 1½ hours. (If you invert the cake before the chips are firm, they will get squashed.)

Run a thin knife around the sides and center tube of the pan to loosen the cake. Remove the cake from the pan by inverting it onto a flat serving plate, then place a wire rack on the bottom of the cake and invert the cake onto the rack so it is right side up. Cool the cake thoroughly on the wire rack.

Slip a large metal spatula under the cake and slide it onto a serving plate. Dust lightly with powdered sugar before serving. Use a large knife to cut the cake into slices.

The cake can be covered and stored at room temperature for up to 3 days.

# strawberry and white chocolate chip cheesecake

Think spring in a cheesecake: a soft pink strawberry filling with creamy white chocolate chips and a dazzling topping of whole strawberries drizzled with white chocolate. This is perfect for those many celebrations of spring—Mother's Day, wedding showers, and graduations.

Soften the cream cheese thoroughly so it will mix smoothly into the batter. A quick method for softening cream cheese is to let the wrapped packages sit in a sunny window just until the cream cheese feels soft if pressed with a finger.

**mixing time** 20 minutes for crust, filling, and topping

**baking** 325° F. for about 1 hour and 15 minutes for the filling, plus 8 minutes for the crust.

### crust

1¾ cups graham cracker crumbs

¾ teaspoon ground cinnamon

7 tablespoons unsalted butter, melted

### filling

3 cups strawberries, washed and stemmed

2 pounds cream cheese, at room temperature

1¼ cups sugar

2 tablespoons unbleached all-purpose flour

4 large eggs, at room temperature

2 teaspoons vanilla extract

½ teaspoon almond extract

2 tablespoons heavy whipping cream

1 cup (5¾ ounces) white chocolate chips

### topping

2 pints (about 34) strawberries, washed and stemmed

½ cup white chocolate chips

1 teaspoon canola or corn oil

continued...

**Make the crust.** Position a rack in the middle of the oven. Preheat the oven to 325°F. Butter a 9-inch springform pan with sides at least 2¾ inches high. Wrap the outside of the pan with a large piece of heavy-duty aluminum foil. Have ready a baking pan with at least 2-inch-high sides that is large enough to hold the springform pan.

In a large bowl, stir the graham cracker crumbs and cinnamon together. Mix in the melted butter until the crumbs are evenly moistened. Scrape the crumb mixture into the prepared pan and press it evenly over the bottom and 1 inch up the sides of the pan. Be careful not to make the crust too thick in the corners of the pan.

Bake the crust for 8 minutes. Set aside on a wire rack, with the oven left on, while you mix the filling.

**Make the filling.** In a food processor, process the strawberries to a puree. Strain the puree into a small bowl, pressing on the solids in the strainer to help push the liquid through the strainer; discard any seeds or pulp left in the strainer. Measure 1 cup of puree for the filling and set aside. If there is any extra puree, save it for another use.

In a large bowl, using an electric mixer on low speed, beat the cream cheese and sugar just until smoothly blended.

Mix in the flour. Lightly beat the eggs in a small bowl, then add them in two additions, beating just to blend them in smoothly. Mix in the vanilla, almond extract, and cream. Mix in the strawberry puree until the batter is evenly pink. Stir in the white chocolate chips.

Pour the batter into the baked crust. Put the pan in the large baking pan and set on the oven rack. Pour enough hot water into the large pan to reach 1 inch up the sides of the springform pan. Bake until the center seems firm when you give the cheesecake a gentle shake, about 1 hour and 15 minutes. When done, the cheesecake may have a few tiny cracks around the edge but these will close up as the cheesecake cools.

Cover the cheesecake loosely with paper towels and let cool in its water bath for 1 hour.

Carefully remove the cheesecake from the water bath. Remove the paper towels and the foil wrapping from the pan and cool the cheesecake on a wire rack for 1 hour, or until it feels cool to the touch.

Cover the cheesecake with plastic wrap and chill in the refrigerator for at least 6 hours, or overnight. The cheesecake will be firm when cool. It can be refrigerated for up to 2 days

before the fresh strawberry topping is added.

**Add the topping.** Arrange the whole strawberries on top of the cheesecake, covering it thickly.

Put the white chocolate chips and oil in a heatproof bowl or the top of a double boiler and place it over a saucepan of barely simmering water (or the bottom of the double boiler); the water should not touch the bowl. Stir until the white chocolate is melted and smooth.

Use a small spoon to drizzle thin, swirling lines of the white chocolate coating over the strawberries. Once the strawberry topping is added, the cheesecake should be served the same day. Refrigerate until ready to serve.

To serve, use a small knife to loosen the cheesecake from the sides of the pan and remove the sides. Use a large sharp knife to cut the cheesecake, carefully wiping the knife clean after each slice.

# in-the-chips marble cake

This all-in-one cake is made of a yellow batter with dark chocolate chips and a chocolate batter with white chocolate chips. Sound complicated? Not at all. It only takes one batter that is divided and flavored differently.

**mixing time** 10 minutes

**baking** 325° F. for about 1 hour and 10 minutes

2¾ cups cake flour

1 teaspoon baking powder

½ teaspoon baking soda

½ teaspoon salt

3 large eggs

2 cups sugar

1 cup canola or corn oil

2 tablespoons dark rum

2 teaspoons vanilla extract

1 cup sour cream

3 tablespoons unsweetened Dutch-process cocoa powder, sifted

1 cup (5¾ ounces) white chocolate chips

1 cup (6 ounces) semisweet chocolate chips

Powdered sugar for dusting

Preheat the oven to 325° F. Oil the bottom, sides, and center tube of a 9½- or 10-inch fixed-bottom tube pan with at least 3¾-inch-high sides. Line the bottom of the pan with a ring of parchment paper and butter the paper.

Sift the flour, baking powder, baking soda, and salt into a medium bowl and set aside.

In a large bowl, using an electric mixer on medium speed, beat the eggs and sugar until thick and lightened to a cream color, about 2 minutes. Stop the mixer and scrape the sides of the bowl as needed during mixing. On low speed, slowly mix in the oil, rum, and vanilla until blended. Add the flour mixture, mixing just until it is incorporated. Mix in the sour cream until no white streaks remain.

Remove 2 cups of the batter to a medium bowl. Stir in the cocoa powder until it is blended into the batter. Stir in the white chocolate chips. Set aside.

Stir the semisweet chocolate chips into the yellow batter remaining in the large bowl. Pour half of the yellow batter into the prepared pan, spread-ing it evenly. Spoon the chocolate batter evenly on top of it and use a small knife to swirl it lightly once through the batter. This marbleizes the batter but keeps the chocolate batter in appealing large sections. Pour the remaining yellow batter into the pan and gently spread it evenly.

Bake until the top looks light brown and a toothpick inserted in the center comes out clean, about 1 hour and 10 minutes. Let the cake cool in the pan on a wire rack for about 30 minutes.

Run a thin knife around the sides and center tube of the pan to loosen the cake. Remove the cake from the pan by inverting it onto a flat serving plate, then place a wire rack on the bottom of the cake and invert the cake onto the rack so it is right side up. Cool the cake thoroughly on the wire rack.

Dust the cake lightly with powdered sugar before serving, and use a large sharp knife to cut the cake into slices.

The cake can be covered and stored at room temperature for up to 3 days.

# hot chocolate chip brownie sundae cake

Picture this: Buried under a scoop of ice cream is your own dish of a warm, half-baked fudgy brownie with warm, melted chocolate chips spilling out of its center. Forget the picture—better just make it right now.

The ramekins can be filled and refrigerated overnight before baking. Cold batter will need to bake for about 25 minutes.

The slightly sunken center of these brownies is just right for holding a scoop of ice cream. Vanilla or vanilla-based flavors pair well with the intensely chocolate cake.

**mixing time** 10 minutes

**baking** 350° F. for about 20 minutes

### cakes

½ cup (1 stick) cold unsalted butter, cut into pieces

1 ounce unsweetened chocolate, chopped

¾ cup (about 4 ounces) plus 2 tablespoons bittersweet chocolate chips

2 large eggs

1 cup sugar

¼ teaspoon salt

1 teaspoon vanilla extract

½ cup unbleached all-purpose flour

About 1½ pints ice cream, such as vanilla, chocolate chip cookie dough, or chocolate chip, for serving

Position a rack in the middle of the oven. Preheat the oven to 350°F. Butter six 6-ounce ramekins or custard cups and put them on a baking sheet. (The baking sheet makes it easier to move the ramekins in and out of the oven.)

Put the butter, unsweetened chocolate, and ½ cup of the chocolate chips in a heatproof bowl or the top of a double boiler and place it over a saucepan of barely simmering water (or the bottom of the double boiler); the water should not touch the bowl. Stir until the butter and chocolate are melted and smooth. Set aside to cool slightly.

In a large bowl, using an electric mixer on medium speed, beat the eggs, sugar, and salt until thickened and the color lightens, about 1 minute. Stop the mixer and scrape the sides of the bowl as needed during mixing. On low speed, mix in the melted chocolate mixture and vanilla until blended. Add the flour, mixing just until it is incorporated.

Divide the batter evenly among the ramekins, about a generous ⅓ cup in each. Put 1 tablespoon of the remaining chocolate chips in the center of each. Use your fingers to press the chips lightly into the batter; it is not necessary to cover the chips completely with batter, as they will sink during baking.

Bake just until the tops look dry and a crisp top has formed, about 20 minutes. Let cool for 15 to 30 minutes.

Top each cake with a large scoop of ice cream and serve.

# chocolate chip cakes with frosting and/or fillings

These cakes, and their frostings and fillings, show off how versatile chocolate chips can be. There is a simple chocolate-glazed gingerbread to tuck in a lunch box, thickly frosted cupcakes to carry to a picnic, and a multilayered meringue and whipped cream cake for a fancy finish to any occasion. Glazes and frostings are made with melted chocolate chips, chocolate chip cookies become the cake part of a trifle, and chocolate chips are used to decorate cakes.

Cakes are baked on the middle rack of the oven, where they are most evenly surrounded by hot air. All ovens are different, so be sure to check cakes as the end of their baking time nears. And as soon as they feel firm on top, check cakes with a toothpick: If the toothpick comes out clean, the cake is done. Some of these cake batters include chocolate chips, so if the toothpick penetrates a chocolate chip, try the toothpick test in another spot. After baking, cakes are usually left in their pans for at least 15 minutes to cool and firm slightly. Then they are turned out of the pans to cool on a wire rack. The wire rack allows cakes to cool evenly and let air to circulate around them so they do not become soggy.

Baking meringues is essentially a drying-out process. They are done when they look dry and feel dry if lightly touched. Letting meringues sit in a turned-off oven for an hour after they bake ensures that they will be dry and crisp but not become too dark.

A smooth finish is what you want from any frosting or filling. For a butter-cream-type frosting, softening the butter or cream cheese is the key to having it combine smoothly with the powdered sugar. Whipped cream only needs to be whipped to a thick, smooth consistency. When whipped softly, the cream will form soft peaks, which you will see when it falls from a spoon.

Cream whipped to firm peaks will form a point that stands straight up and remains that way when the beater or whisk is lifted. If cream is overwhipped, it will look grainy. If this should happen, whisking in a little more cold cream a tablespoon at a time can often smooth out overwhipped cream. Better yet, keep a close watch on cream when whipping it and stop whipping as soon as the desired stage is reached. Cakes with whipped cream must be stored in the refrigerator and are always served cold.

Melting the chocolate for a glaze over gentle heat produces smoothly melted chocolate and, in turn, a smooth, shiny glaze. Glazes need to cool to a consistency that is thick enough to cling to a cake.

A thin metal spatula is the best tool for spreading frosting or filling smoothly over a cake. If any cake crumbs adhere to the spatula, wipe the spatula clean on the edge of the frosting bowl before taking a new dollop of frosting.

Most frosted cakes can be made in stages. Bake the cake the day before serving it. Cover the cooled cake and let it sit at room temperature. Then make the frosting and/or filling the following day and assemble or finish the cake. These two shorter processes seem to fit quite easily into my schedule.

# pumpkin chocolate chip cake with cream cheese frosting

My friend Dianne Hannan's pumpkin chocolate chip cookies introduced me to that great combination and inspired this cake. It is a dark golden pumpkin cake that is studded with chocolate chips and topped off with a white cream cheese frosting.

Check to make sure that the label on the can of pumpkin says "pumpkin" rather than "pumpkin pie filling," which has spices added.

**mixing time** 15 minutes for cake
and frosting
**baking** 325° F. for about 40 minutes

## cake

1½ cups unbleached all-purpose flour
¾ teaspoon baking powder
¾ teaspoon baking soda
½ teaspoon salt
1½ teaspoons ground cinnamon
¾ teaspoon ground ginger
1 cup canned pumpkin
1 cup sugar
½ cup canola or corn oil
2 large eggs
2 cups (12 ounces) semisweet
chocolate chips

## frosting

½ cup (1 stick) unsalted butter,
at room temperature
4 ounces cream cheese, at room
temperature
1 teaspoon vanilla extract
1¾ cups powdered sugar

**continued...**

**Make the cake.** Position a rack in the middle of the oven. Preheat the oven to 325° F. Butter a 9-inch square baking pan. Line the bottom of the pan with parchment paper and butter the paper.

Sift the flour, baking powder, baking soda, salt, cinnamon, and ginger into a medium bowl and set aside.

In a large bowl, using an electric mixer on medium speed, beat the pumpkin, sugar, and oil until smoothly blended, about 1 minute. Stop the mixer and scrape the sides of the bowl as needed during mixing. Mix in the eggs one at a time until blended into the batter. On low speed, add the flour mixture, mixing just until it is incorporated. Mix in the chocolate chips until evenly distributed.

Scrape the batter into the prepared pan. Bake just until the top feels firm and a toothpick inserted in the center comes out clean, about 40 minutes. If the toothpick penetrates a chocolate chip, test another spot. Transfer the pan to a wire rack to cool for 20 minutes.

Loosen the sides of the cake from the sides of the pan and invert it onto the wire rack. Remove and discard the paper liner and let the cake cool completely.

**Make the frosting.** In a large bowl, using an electric mixer on low speed, beat the butter, cream cheese, and vanilla until thoroughly blended and smooth, about 1 minute. Stop the mixer and scrape the sides of the bowl. Add the powdered sugar, mixing until smooth, about 1 minute, then beat on medium speed for about 1 minute to lighten the frosting.

Place a serving plate on the cooled cake and invert the cake onto it so it is right side up.

Use a thin metal spatula to spread the frosting smoothly over the top of the cake.

Use a large sharp knife to cut the cake into 12 squares.

The frosted cake can be covered and stored in the refrigerator for up to 3 days. Let it stand at room temperature for about 1 hour before serving.

# chocolate chip gingerbread

I don't know why I didn't think of this sooner, but I'm glad that I finally did try adding chocolate chips to spicy gingerbread. Then I took the ginger and chocolate idea to the limit and topped the cake off with a chocolate glaze. As with most gingerbread, the flavors develop over time, and the cake tastes even better the next day.

**mixing time** 15 minutes for cake and glaze

**baking** 350° F. for about 30 minutes

2 cups unbleached all-purpose flour

1 teaspoon baking powder

¹/₂ teaspoon baking soda

¹/₄ teaspoon salt

1 teaspoon ground cinnamon

1 tablespoon ground ginger

6 tablespoons (³/₄ stick) unsalted butter, melted

³/₄ cup packed light brown sugar

2 large eggs

¹/₃ cup molasses

1 cup strong coffee, cooled

2 cups (12 ounces) semisweet chocolate chips

1 cup Chocolate Glaze (page 92), cooled until thick enough to spread

Position a rack in the middle of the oven. Preheat the oven to 350°F. Butter a 9-inch square baking pan. Line the bottom of the pan with parchment paper and butter the paper.

Sift the flour, baking powder, baking soda, salt, cinnamon, and ginger into a medium bowl and set aside.

In a large bowl, using an electric mixer on medium speed, beat the melted butter, brown sugar, eggs, and molasses until smoothly blended, about 1 minute. Stop the mixer and scrape the sides of the bowl as needed during mixing. On low speed, add the flour mixture in 3 additions and the coffee in 2 additions, beginning and ending with the flour mixture and mixing just until the flour is incorporated. Mix in the chocolate chips until evenly distributed.

Scrape the batter into the prepared pan. Bake just until the top feels firm and a toothpick inserted in the center comes out clean, about 30 minutes. If

the toothpick penetrates a chocolate chip, test another spot. Transfer the pan to a wire rack to cool for 20 minutes.

Loosen the sides of the cake from the sides of the pan and invert it onto the wire rack. Remove and discard the paper liner, and let the cake cool completely.

Place a serving plate on the cooled cake and invert the cake onto it so it is right side up. Use a thin metal spatula to spread the glaze smoothly over the top of the gingerbread.

Use a large sharp knife to cut the cake into 12 squares to serve.

The gingerbread can be covered and stored at room temperature for up to 2 days.

# chocolate chip cupcakes with thick fudge frosting

For years I have been searching for a not too sweet, easy dark fudge frosting for cupcakes and brownies. It was right under my nose all the time. Turns out that when I made a few ingredient adjustments (like adding more chocolate chips) to the truffle mixture that I make regularly, it produces a fudge frosting. I slathered mounds of it on these chocolate chip cupcakes and ended my search.

**mixing time** 15 minutes for cupcakes
 and frosting
**baking** 350° F. for about 24 minutes

**cupcakes**

1¼ cups cake flour
1 teaspoon baking powder
¼ teaspoon salt
½ cup (1 stick) unsalted butter,
 at room temperature
1 cup sugar
2 large eggs
1 teaspoon vanilla extract
½ cup whole milk
1 cup (6 ounces) semisweet
 chocolate chips

**frosting**

1 cup heavy whipping cream
½ teaspoon instant coffee powder
¼ cup (½ stick) unsalted butter,
 cut into 8 pieces
2 cups (12 ounces) semisweet
 chocolate chips
1 cup (5¾ ounces) bittersweet
 chocolate chips
1 teaspoon vanilla extract

**Make the cupcakes.** Position a rack in the middle of the oven. Preheat the oven to 350° F. Line 12 muffin tin cups with paper cupcake liners.

Sift the cake flour, baking powder, and salt into a medium bowl and set aside.

In a large bowl, using an electric mixer on medium speed, beat the butter and sugar until smoothly blended and creamy, about 2 minutes. Stop the mixer and scrape the sides of the bowl as needed during mixing. Add the eggs one at a time, mixing until each is blended into the batter. Add the vanilla and beat for 1 more minute. The mixture may look slightly curdled. On low speed, add half of the flour mixture, mixing just until it is incorporated. Mix in the milk until blended. Mix in the remaining flour mixture just until it is incorporated. Mix in the chocolate chips.

Fill each paper liner with ¼ cup of batter, to about ½ inch below the top. Bake just until the tops feel firm and a toothpick inserted in the center comes out clean, about 24 minutes. If the toothpick penetrates a chocolate chip, test another spot. Cool the cupcakes for 10 minutes in the pan on a wire rack.

Carefully place a wire rack on top of the pan of cupcakes. Protecting your hands with pot holders and holding the pan and rack together, invert them to release the cupcakes onto the wire rack. Turn the cupcakes right side up to cool completely.

**Make the frosting.** In a medium saucepan, stir the cream and coffee together to dissolve the coffee. Add the butter pieces and heat over low heat until the cream is hot and the butter melts. The mixture should form tiny bubbles and measure about 175° F. on an instant-read thermometer; do not let the mixture boil, or it may form a skin on top. (If this does happen, use a spoon to carefully lift off the skin and discard it.) Remove the pan from the heat, add the semisweet and bittersweet chocolate chips, and let them sit in the hot cream mixture for about 30 seconds to soften, then whisk just until all of the chocolate is melted and the filling is smooth. If necessary, return the saucepan to low heat for 1 to 2 minutes, stirring constantly, to melt the chocolate chips completely. Stir in the vanilla.

Pour the chocolate mixture into a large bowl. Let sit at room temperature until the frosting thickens enough for a spoon to stand upright in it, about 2 hours. Or, press a piece of plastic wrap onto the frosting, poke a few small holes in the wrap with the tip of a knife to let steam escape, and refrigerate until the mixture thickens to a spreadable consistency, about 45 minutes. Stir the frosting every 15 minutes to make sure that it thickens evenly.

Use a small spatula to spread a scant ¼ cup of frosting on top of each cupcake, mounding the frosting in the center.

The cupcakes can be covered and stored at room temperature for up to 2 days.

# chocolate-banana whipped cream trifle

Lavish, impressive, and generous, this trifle has multiple layers of Banana-Oatmeal Chocolate Chip Cookies, sliced bananas, chocolate, and whipped cream. If you have the cookies baked and ready in the freezer, it takes only minutes to put it together. For the traditional presentation, assemble the trifle in a glass serving bowl so the many layers show through.

**mixing time** 15 minutes

⅔ cup (about 4 ounces) bittersweet chocolate chips

**whipped cream**

2 cups cold heavy whipping cream

½ cup powdered sugar

1 tablespoon dark rum

1 teaspoon vanilla extract

4 large or 5 medium ripe bananas, sliced

16 Banana-Oatmeal Chocolate Chip Cookies (page 25; defrosted if frozen)

Have ready a bowl with a 2½- to 3-quart capacity, preferably glass.

Put the chocolate chips in a heatproof bowl or the top of a double boiler and place it over a saucepan of barely simmering water (or the bottom of the double boiler); the water should not touch the bowl. Stir until the chocolate is melted and smooth. Set aside to cool slightly.

**Make the whipped cream.** In a large bowl, using an electric mixer on medium-high speed, beat the cream, powdered sugar, rum, and vanilla until firm peaks form.

To assemble the trifle, spread about 1 cup of the whipped cream over the bottom of the bowl. Spread one-third of the banana slices over the cream. Use a small spoon to drizzle about 2 teaspoons of the melted chocolate chips over the bananas. Add a layer of 4 cookies, breaking them up to fit if necessary. Repeat the layering of whipped cream, bananas, chocolate,

and cookies to make 2 more layers. Add a fourth layer of whipped cream. Break the remaining 4 cookies into pieces about 1 inch in size and scatter them over the whipped cream. Drizzle the remaining melted chocolate chips over the cookies.

Refrigerate the trifle for about 15 minutes to firm up the chocolate topping, then cover carefully with plastic wrap and refrigerate for at least 3 hours, or overnight. Serve cold.

Use a large spoon to serve the trifle, digging down through the layers to the bottom of the bowl for each serving.

# chocolate-covered chocolate chip cake

When my niece, Rachel Ossakow, tested this cake for me, she liked it so much that she made it twice in one weekend to serve to two different groups of friends. It was a case of having parties so she could make the cake again—and again. The moist yellow cake has a triple hit of chocolate chips: It is studded with chocolate chips, covered with a chocolate glaze made with bittersweet chocolate chips, and decorated with chocolate chips pressed onto the sides.

**mixing time** 15 minutes for cake
  and glaze
**baking** 350° F. for about 1 hour

### cake
3 cups cake flour
1 teaspoon baking powder
1/2 teaspoon baking soda
1/2 teaspoon salt
3 large eggs
2 cups sugar
1 cup canola or corn oil
2 teaspoons vanilla extract
1 cup sour cream
1 cup (6 ounces) semisweet
  chocolate chips

### chocolate glaze
1/3 cup heavy whipping cream
1/4 cup (1/2 stick) unsalted butter,
  cut into pieces at room temperature
2 tablespoons corn syrup
1 cup (5 3/4 ounces) bittersweet
  chocolate chips
2 cups (12 ounces) regular or miniature
  semisweet chocolate chips

**Make the cake.** Position a rack in the middle of the oven. Preheat the oven to 350°F. Butter the bottom and sides of a fixed-bottom 9½- or 10-inch tube pan with at least 3¾-inch-high sides. Line the bottom of the pan with a ring of parchment and butter the paper.

Sift the flour, baking powder, baking soda, and salt into a medium bowl and set aside.

In a large bowl, using an electric mixer on medium speed, beat the eggs and sugar at medium speed until fluffy, thick, and lightened in color, about 2 minutes. Reduce the speed to low and mix in the oil and vanilla until blended. Add the flour mixture, mixing just to incorporate it. Mix in the sour cream until no white streaks remain. Mix in the chocolate chips.

Scrape the batter into the prepared pan. Bake until a toothpick inserted in the center comes out clean or with just a few crumbs attached, about 1 hour. If the toothpick penetrates a chocolate chip, test another spot. Cool the cake in the pan on a wire rack for 15 minutes.

Use a small sharp knife to loosen the cake from the sides and center tube of the pan. Place a wire rack on the top of the cake and invert the cake onto it. Carefully remove the paper liner, and leave the cake bottom side up to cool completely.

**Make the chocolate glaze.** Combine the cream, butter, and corn syrup in a medium saucepan and heat over medium heat until the cream is hot and the butter melts. The mixture should form tiny bubbles and measure about 175° F. on an instant-read thermometer; do not let the mixture boil, or it may form a skin on top. (If this does happen, use a spoon to carefully lift off the skin and discard it.) Remove from the heat, add the bittersweet chocolate chips, and let them sit in the hot cream mixture for about 1 minute, then whisk just until all of the chocolate is melted and the glaze is smooth. Set aside for about 20 minutes to cool and thicken slightly so the glaze will cling to the cake.

Use a small spatula to spread the glaze over the top and sides and inside the center hole of the cooled cake. Let the glaze set and firm up for about 15 minutes, then press the semisweet chocolate chips onto the sides of cake.

The cake can be covered and stored at room temperature for up to 3 days.

# chocolate chip angel cake with chocolate marshmallow frosting

Think clouds—chocolate clouds, that is—and you will be able to imagine this cake. It is a lighter-than-air angel food cake made moist with tiny chocolate chips, finished with a billowy chocolate seven-minute frosting.

Angel food cake is baked in an ungreased tube pan so that during baking, the cake rises slowly up the sides and center tube of the pan and hugs the ungreased surface firmly. Nonstick pans should not be used.

**mixing time** 25 minutes for cake and frosting
**baking** 325° F. for about 45 minutes

### cake

1 cup cake flour
1³/₄ cups sugar
1³/₄ cups large egg whites (about 11 large eggs)
1 teaspoon cream of tartar
¹/₄ teaspoon salt
2 teaspoons vanilla extract
¹/₂ teaspoon almond extract
1¹/₂ cups (9 ounces) miniature semisweet chocolate chips

### frosting

¹/₂ cup (about 3 ounces) bittersweet chocolate chips
1¹/₄ cups sugar
¹/₃ cup water
3 large egg whites
¹/₄ teaspoon cream of tartar
1 teaspoon vanilla extract
¹/₄ teaspoon almond extract

**continued...**

**Make the cake.** Position a rack in the middle of the oven. Preheat the oven to 325° F. Have ready a 9½- or 10-inch tube pan with at least 3¾-inch-high sides; do not use a nonstick pan. If the pan does not have a removable bottom, line the bottom with a ring of parchment or wax paper.

Sift the flour and ¾ cup of the sugar into a medium bowl and set aside.

In a large bowl, using an electric mixer on low speed, beat the egg whites, cream of tartar, and salt until the whites are foamy and the cream of tartar dissolves. On medium speed, beat until the egg whites look shiny and smooth and the movement of the beaters forms lines in the beaten whites. If you stop the mixer and lift up the beaters, the whites should cling to the beaters. Slowly beat in the remaining 1 cup of sugar, 2 table-spoons at a time, then beat to firm, glossy peaks, about 1 minute. Mix in the vanilla and almond extract. On low speed, mix in the flour mixture, sprin-kling ⅓ cup of the mixture at a time over the egg whites and incorporating each addition before adding more. Use a rubber spatula to fold in the choco-late chips. Scrape the batter into the tube pan.

Bake until the top of the cake is golden and feels firm when gently pressed,

about 45 minutes. Invert the pan onto a narrow-necked bottle (a full wine bottle works well) to cool thoroughly, about 1½ hours.

Remove the pan from the bottle and run a thin knife around the sides and center tube of the pan to loosen the cake. Remove the cake from the pan by inverting it onto a flat serving plate. Leave the cake bottom side up. Tuck waxed paper strips just an inch or so under the cake all the way around to keep the plate clean.

**Make the frosting.** Put the chocolate chips in a heatproof bowl or the top of a double boiler and place it over a saucepan of barely simmering water (or the bottom of the double boiler); the water should not touch the bowl. Stir until the chocolate chips are melted and smooth. Set aside to cool slightly.

Put the sugar, water, egg whites, and cream of tartar in a heatproof bowl or the (clean) top of a double boiler with at least a 2-quart capacity and beat with a handheld electric mixer on high speed until opaque, white, and foamy, about 1 minute. Put the bowl over a saucepan of barely simmering water (or the bottom of the double boiler); the water should not touch the bowl and the top container should sit firmly over the pan of hot water. Beat on

high speed (be sure to keep the mixer cord away from the burner) until a soft point that stands straight up forms if you stop the beaters and lift them out of the mixture, about 7 minutes. The mixture will register 160° F. on an instant-read thermometer. Remove the bowl from the water, add the melted chocolate, vanilla, and almond extract, and beat for 2 minutes to thicken the frosting.

Use a thin metal spatula to spread the frosting generously over the top and sides and inside center hole of the cake. To form swirls, dip the spatula gently into the frosting and lift it up. Remove the wax paper strips and discard them.

Use a serrated knife for cutting the cake.

The cake can be carefully covered (see page 19) and refrigerated overnight.

# mocha chip meringue cake

This fancy cake has party written all over it. The crisp chocolate chocolate chip meringue layers are filled with coffee and chocolate whipped cream and frosted with chocolate whipped cream. Crushed pieces of meringue make a decorative topping. The cake can be put together a day ahead of time, ready and waiting to appear as the grand finale.

**mixing time** 20 minutes for cake and
   whipped cream
**baking** 275° F. for about 1 hour

### cake

1 cup powdered sugar
3 tablespoons unsweetened
   Dutch-process cocoa powder
5 large egg whites, at room
   temperature
1/4 teaspoon cream of tartar
2/3 cup granulated sugar
1 cup (6 ounces) miniature semisweet
   chocolate chips

### chocolate whipped cream

1/3 cup bittersweet chocolate chips
1 1/2 cups cold heavy whipping cream
1/4 cup powdered sugar
3 tablespoons unsweetened
   Dutch-process cocoa powder
1 teaspoon vanilla extract

### coffee whipped cream

3/4 cup cold heavy whipping cream
2 teaspoons instant coffee powder
1/4 cup powdered sugar
1 teaspoon vanilla extract

Powdered sugar for dusting

**continued...**

**Make the cake.** Position the racks in the middle and upper third of the oven. Preheat the oven to 275° F. Cut 2 pieces of parchment paper to fit 2 baking sheets. Trace two 8-inch circles on one piece and one 8-inch circle on the other piece. Line the baking sheets with the parchment, marked side down.

Sift the powdered sugar and cocoa powder into a small bowl. Set aside.

In a large bowl, using an electric mixer on low speed, beat the egg whites and cream of tartar until the whites are foamy and the cream of tartar dissolves. On medium speed, beat until the egg whites look shiny and smooth and the movement of the beaters forms lines in the beaten whites. If you stop the mixer and lift up the beaters, the whites should cling to the beaters. Slowly beat in the granulated sugar, 2 tablespoons at a time, then beat for about 1 minute. With the mixer on low speed, sprinkle the powdered sugar mixture over the egg whites and mix in. Use a rubber spatula to gently fold in the chocolate chips.

Use a thin metal spatula to spread about 1¼ cups of the meringue mixture in each marked circle. You will use about three-quarters of the meringue mixture for the circles. Spread the remaining meringue mixture in a free-form shape about ½ inch thick on the baking sheet that has the single

meringue. This meringue will be crushed after baking to garnish the top of the cake.

Bake until the meringues feel crisp and dry if touched lightly, about 1 hour. Turn off the oven and leave the meringues in the oven for 1 hour.

Remove the baking sheets from the oven and cool the meringues completely on the baking sheets, about 30 minutes.

**Make the chocolate whipped cream.** Put the chocolate in a large heatproof bowl or the top of a double boiler and place it over a saucepan of barely simmering water (or the bottom of the double boiler); the water should not touch the bowl. Stir until the chocolate is melted and smooth. Remove from the water, scrape the chocolate into a large bowl if you used a double boiler, and set aside to cool slightly while you make the coffee whipped cream.

**Make the coffee whipped cream.** In a large bowl, using an electric mixer on medium-high speed, beat the cream, coffee powder, powdered sugar, and vanilla until firm peaks form. (The coffee will dissolve as the cream whips.) Set aside.

In a clean large bowl, using clean beaters, beat the cream, powdered sugar, cocoa powder, and vanilla on medium-high speed until soft peaks form. Whisk about 1 cup of the

whipped cream into the chocolate until smoothly blended. Use a rubber spatula to fold in the remaining whipped cream.

Spread a tablespoon of chocolate whipped cream in the center of a plate or cardboard cake circle to prevent the cake from sliding around on the plate. Place a meringue layer smooth side down on the plate. Use a thin metal spatula to spread about 1 cup of the chocolate whipped cream evenly over the meringue. Top with another meringue layer and spread the coffee whipped cream over it. Top the cake with the remaining meringue layer, top side up. Spread the remaining chocolate whipped cream evenly over the top of the cake.

Use your hands to crush the meringue for the garnish into pieces up to ½ inch in size and sprinkle them over the top of the cake. Sift powdered sugar lightly over the top of the cake.

Use a large sharp knife to cut the cake into slices.

The cake can be covered and refrigerated overnight.

# chocolate-chocolate chip layer cake with chocolate frosting

Light the candles, scoop the ice cream, and get ready to celebrate. Here is the cake that my daughter-in-law Kate makes (and we look forward to) for family birthday parties—kids and adults alike. Brown sugar and chocolate chips make the cake extra moist. The cake is slathered inside and out with an exceptionally creamy and easily mixed chocolate frosting.

**mixing time** 20 minutes for cake and frosting

**baking** 350° F. for about 35 minutes

### cake

3 ounces unsweetened chocolate, chopped

2 cups unbleached all-purpose flour

2 teaspoons baking soda

½ teaspoon salt

1 cup (2 sticks) unsalted butter, at room temperature

2 cups packed light brown sugar

3 large eggs

2 teaspoons vanilla extract

¾ cup buttermilk

¾ cup hot water

2 cups (12 ounces) semisweet chocolate chips

### frosting

2 ounces unsweetened chocolate, chopped

1 cup (about 5¾ ounces) bittersweet chocolate chips

½ cup heavy whipping cream, at room temperature

1½ teaspoons instant coffee powder

1 cup (2 sticks) unsalted butter, at room temperature

3 cups powdered sugar

2 teaspoons vanilla extract

1 cup (6 ounces) semisweet chocolate chips

Vanilla or coffee ice cream for serving (optional)

**Make the cake.** Position a rack in the middle of the oven. Preheat the oven to 350° F. Butter two 9-inch round cake pans with 1¾- to 2-inch-high sides. Line the bottom of each pan with parchment paper and butter the paper.

Put the unsweetened chocolate in a heatproof bowl or the top of a double boiler and place it over a saucepan of barely simmering water (or the bottom of the double boiler); the water should not touch the bowl. Stir until the chocolate is melted and smooth. Remove from the water and set aside to cool slightly.

Sift the flour, baking soda, and salt into a medium bowl and set aside.

In a large bowl, using an electric mixer on medium speed, beat the butter and brown sugar until smoothly blended and creamy, about 2 minutes. Stop the mixer and scrape the sides of the

**continued...**

bowl as needed during mixing. Add the eggs one at a time, mixing until each is blended into the batter. Add the vanilla and beat for 2 more minutes. On low speed, mix in the melted chocolate. Add the flour mixture in 3 additions and the buttermilk in 2 additions, beginning and ending with the flour and mixing just until it is incorporated. Mix in the hot water just to blend it into the batter. Mix in the chocolate chips.

Scrape the batter into the prepared pans, dividing it evenly. Bake just until the tops feel firm if lightly touched and a toothpick inserted in the center comes out clean, about 35 minutes. If the toothpick penetrates a chocolate chip, test another spot. Cool the layers for 10 minutes in the pans on a wire rack.

Use a small sharp knife to loosen the cake layers from the sides of the pans. Place a wire rack on the top of each cake and invert the cake onto it. Carefully remove the paper liners, then replace the paper loosely on each layer. Let the cake layers cool thoroughly, then discard the liners.

**Make the frosting.** Put the chopped chocolate and chocolate chips in a heatproof bowl or the top of a double boiler and place it over a saucepan of barely simmering water (or the bottom of the double boiler); the water should not touch the bowl. Stir until the chocolate is melted and smooth. Remove from the water and set aside to cool slightly.

In a small bowl, stir the cream and coffee together until the coffee dissolves.

In a large bowl, using an electric mixer on medium speed, beat the butter and powdered sugar until smoothly blended and creamy, about 1 minute. On low speed, beat in the melted chocolate, coffee mixture, and vanilla to blend them into the frosting. On medium speed, beat the frosting until it is fluffy and lightens slightly in color, about 1 minute.

Place a serving plate on the bottom of a cake layer and invert the cake onto it so it is right side up. Tuck waxed paper strips just an inch or so under the cake all the way around to keep the plate clean. Use a thin metal spatula to spread about $1\frac{1}{2}$ cups of frosting over the top of the cake layer, spreading it to the edges. Invert the second layer onto a plate and slide it right side up onto the first layer. Spread the remaining frosting over the top and sides of the cake. Remove the wax paper strips and discard them.

Cut 2 wax paper strips that are $1\frac{1}{2}$ inches wide and 12 inches long.

Lay them across the top of the cake, placing them 2 inches from either side of the cake and spacing them 2 inches apart, so you have 3 strips of frosting visible. Scatter the semisweet chocolate chips over the frosting. Carefully lift up and remove the wax paper strips. You will have a pattern of chocolate chip stripes on top of the cake.

Use a large sharp knife to slice the cake. Serve it with scoops of ice cream, if desired.

The frosted cake can be carefully covered (see page 19) and refrigerated for up to 2 days. Let the cake sit at room temperature for 30 minutes before serving it.

# orange chocolate chip bundt cake

Melissa McDaniel has been one of my testers and most loyal baking fans for years. But she was always the tester, never the creator. For this book, she was determined to create and contribute a recipe. Her moist orange and chocolate chip Bundt cake, drizzled thickly with chocolate glaze, definitely takes the cake.

**mixing time** 15 minutes for cake
  and glaze

**baking** 325° F. for about 65 minutes

2¾ cups unbleached all-purpose flour

1 teaspoon baking powder

½ teaspoon baking soda

½ teaspoon salt

4 large eggs

2 cups sugar

1 cup canola or corn oil

2 teaspoons finely grated orange zest

3 tablespoons Cointreau or other
  orange-flavored liqueur

2 teaspoons vanilla extract

¼ cup fresh orange juice

1 cup sour cream

1 cup (6 ounces) miniature semisweet
  chocolate chips

1 recipe Chocolate Glaze (page 92),
  cooled until slightly thickened

Position a rack in the middle of the oven. Preheat the oven to 325° F. Butter a 12-cup-capacity Bundt pan, then sprinkle flour lightly inside the pan and tilt the pan to coat it with flour. Discard any loose flour.

Sift the flour, baking powder, baking soda, and salt into a medium bowl and set aside.

In a large bowl, using an electric mixer on medium speed, beat the eggs and sugar until fluffy, thick, and lightened in color, about 2 minutes. On low speed, mix in the oil, orange zest, Cointreau, and vanilla until blended. Add half of the flour mixture, mixing just to incorporate it. Mix in the orange juice until blended, then add the remaining flour mixture, mixing just to incorporate it. Mix in the sour cream until no white streaks remain. Stir in the chocolate chips.

Scrape the batter into the prepared pan. Bake until a toothpick inserted in the center comes out clean or with just a few crumbs attached, about 65 minutes. If a toothpick penetrates a chocolate chip, test another spot. Cool the cake in the pan on a wire rack for 15 minutes.

Use a small sharp knife to loosen the cake from the sides and center tube of the pan. Invert the cake onto a wire rack; tap the bottom of the pan several times if it does not release immediately. Remove the pan and cool the cake completely.

Use a spoon to drizzle the glaze over the top of the cake, letting it drip down the sides. Use a large knife to slice the cake. The cake can be carefully covered and left at room temperature for two days.

**Choices** Bake the cake in a tube pan. Butter the inside of a fixed-bottom 9½- or 10-inch tube pan with at least 3¾-inch-high sides. Line the bottom with a ring of parchment paper and butter the paper. Proceed with the recipe as directed and leave the cake bottom side up for glazing.

# chocolate chip ice cream desserts

I was raised in a family that served ice cream every night, so it was no wonder that when I grew up, I started creating desserts from ice cream. When my mom, who was a great baker, gave my ice cream creations the supreme compliment of calling them "better than a hot fudge sundae," I knew I was on to a "cool" thing.

Ice cream desserts are simple to make. They can be made completely or partially ahead of time and take only minutes to assemble. An ice cream loaf or bombe, for example, needs to be made hours or even days ahead. Sauces can be made in advance and warmed up at serving time. Whether you are serving two or twenty, quantities for these ice cream desserts can be adjusted down or up to fit your crowd.

Supermarket freezers now carry so many flavors and brands of ice cream that a trip to the local market is as far as you need to go for ingredients. Good-quality, rather than premium, ice cream is the best choice for these desserts. Premium ice creams are excessively rich for them.

When spreading ice cream in a crust, in a pan, or on a cookie, it must be soft. A good softening method is to let the ice cream sit in the refrigerator for about 30 minutes. Do not let it melt. If ice cream melts, the air that was churned into it is lost and the result may be a hard, icy texture when the ice cream refreezes. Be sure to cool any crusts or cookies thoroughly so that they do not melt your carefully softened ice cream.

An ice cream loaf or cake softens slightly and cuts easily if it sits for about 5 minutes at room temperature. Always return any leftover ice cream desserts to the freezer promptly to prevent melting.

# girdle-buster ice cream pie

When I was a teenager growing up in central Florida, my mom and I used to take shopping trips to Winter Park. I wasn't that interested in shopping, but I always went along for the Girdle-Buster Ice Cream Pie. It was served in a tiny courtyard restaurant whose name I forgot long ago, but I've never forgotten that dessert. I remembered it as an extravagant coffee dessert, but when I decided to re-create it, I realized that all I had to do was fill a graham cracker–chocolate chip crumb crust with coffee ice cream and "frost" it with fudge sauce.

**mixing time** 10 minutes
**baking** 325° F. for 6 minutes

**crust**

1½ cups graham cracker crumbs

5 tablespoons unsalted butter, melted

⅔ cup (4 ounces) miniature semisweet chocolate chips

2 pints coffee ice cream, softened just until spreadable

1½ cups Fudge Sauce (page 114), warmed just until spreadable

**Make the crust.** Position a rack in the middle of the oven. Preheat the oven to 325° F. Butter a 9-inch pie pan.

In a large bowl, stir the graham cracker crumbs and melted butter together until the crumbs are evenly moistened. Mix in the chocolate chips.

Press the crust mixture evenly over the bottom and up the sides of the pie pan. Bake for 6 minutes. Let the crust cool thoroughly, about 45 minutes.

Use an ice cream spade or a rubber spatula to spread the coffee ice cream in the cooled crust. Smooth the top. Freeze until the ice cream is firm, about 1 hour.

Pour the fudge sauce over the ice cream. Use a thin metal spatula to spread it evenly over the top, completely covering the ice cream. Freeze

the pie for about 30 minutes to firm the sauce.

Wrap the pie, in its pan, tightly in plastic wrap and then heavy-duty aluminum foil. Freeze overnight, or for up to 1 week.

To serve the pie, remove it from the freezer, unwrap it, and use a large sharp knife to cut the pie into slices.

# chocolate chip cookie crunch and peppermint ice cream loaf

Stripes of peppermint and vanilla ice cream separated by crisp chunks of chocolate-coated cookie crumbs make a dessert that has holiday season written all over it. The crunch is made by coating crumbs of Chock-Full of Chocolate Chip Cookies with melted bittersweet chocolate chips. When baking a batch of the cookies, cool, wrap, and freeze eight cookies to use for this loaf.

**mixing time** 15 minutes

**crunch**

8 Chock-Full of Chocolate Chip Cookies (page 24)

²/₃ cup (about 4 ounces) bittersweet chocolate chips

1 tablespoon corn or canola oil

2 pints peppermint ice cream, softened just until spreadable

1 pint vanilla ice cream, softened just until spreadable

1¹/₂ cups Fudge Sauce (page 114), warmed just until pourable

**continued...**

Line a 9-by-5-by-3-inch loaf pan with a piece of parchment paper that is long enough to extend over the two long sides of the pan.

**Make the cookie crunch.** Break each cookie into about 5 pieces. In a food processor, using on/off bursts, process the cookies to crumbs. You should have about 2 cups of cookie crumbs. Put the cookies in a large bowl and set aside.

Put the bittersweet chocolate chips and oil in a heatproof bowl or the top of a double boiler and place it over a saucepan of barely simmering water (or the bottom of the double boiler); the water should not touch the bowl. Stir until the chocolate is melted and smooth.

Pour the chocolate coating over the cookie crumbs, stirring until the crumbs are coated evenly with chocolate. The mixture will look shiny and form pieces of crunch that vary in size from about $1/4$ to $1/2$ inch. The crunch will change from shiny to dull and become crisp as it cools.

Put 1 cup of the crunch in a container, cover it tightly, and reserve it to garnish the top of the ice cream loaf. Use an ice cream spade or the back of a spoon to spread 1 pint of the peppermint ice cream in an even layer over the bottom of the loaf pan, spreading it carefully to the edges. Spoon 1 cup of the crunch over the ice cream. Spread the vanilla ice cream over

the crunch and spoon the remaining crunch over the ice cream. Spread the remaining peppermint ice cream over the crunch. Fold the edges of he parchment over the top of the loaf and cover tightly with plastic wrap. Freeze for at least 5 hours, or up to 1 week.

To serve, chill a serving plate for about 15 minutes. Remove the loaf from the freezer and unwrap it. Use a thin sharp knife to loosen the ice cream from the unlined ends of the pan. Dip a dish towel in hot water, wring it out, and press the hot towel against the sides of the pan for about 25 seconds. Fold back the edges of the parchment, place the chilled serving plate on top of the loaf, and, pulling on the edges of the parchment paper, invert the loaf onto the plate. Remove and discard the paper liner. Press the reserved 1 cup of crunch onto the top of the loaf.

Use a large sharp knife to cut the ice cream loaf into slices a scant 1 inch thick. Pass warm fudge sauce to pour over each serving.

**Choices** Substitute mint chocolate chip ice cream for the peppermint ice cream, or try a pint each of peppermint, chocolate, and vanilla. Chocolate and coffee ice cream is another good combination.

# caramel fudge sundaes

Wondrous things happen when you cook plain old granulated sugar to a dark golden caramel color and add cream to make caramel sauce. Adding chocolate chips to the warm caramel sauce creates a super version that has all the qualities of a hot fudge sauce enhanced with the flavor of caramel.

Remember that caramel is very hot, and be careful not to splash any of the hot mixture on yourself.

**cooking time** 10 minutes

**sauce**

¾ cup heavy whipping cream

½ cup water

1 cup sugar

½ teaspoon vanilla extract

¼ cup bittersweet chocolate chips

2 pints vanilla ice cream

**Make the sauce.** Put the cream in a small saucepan and warm it over low heat. Adjust the heat to keep the cream warm while you cook the sugar.

Combine the water and sugar in a heavy-bottomed saucepan with at least a 3-quart capacity, cover the pan, and cook over low-medium heat until the sugar dissolves, about 6 minutes. Uncover the pan occasionally and brush down any sugar crystals that have formed on the sides with a wet pastry brush. Remove the cover, increase the heat to medium-high, and bring the mixture to a boil. Boil until it turns a dark golden color, tilting the pan occasionally to ensure that the sugar cooks evenly, about 10 minutes. Once the caramel begins to change color, it will reach the dark golden stage quickly, so watch it carefully and remove it from the heat immediately when it is ready.

Use a wooden spoon to slowly stir the hot cream into the hot caramelized sugar. The mixture will bubble up, so be careful. Stir the cream and caramel together until they are smoothly combined. Set the sauce aside for 5 minutes to cool.

Add the vanilla and chocolate chips to the sauce, stirring until the chocolate melts.

Scoop or spoon the ice cream into 6 goblets, sundae dishes, or shallow bowls. Spoon the warm caramel fudge sauce generously over each serving.

The sauce can be cooled, covered, and refrigerated for up to 1 week. Reheat it over low heat until it is soft and pourable.

**Choices** Feel free to substitute other ice cream flavors.

# two-bite-size milk chocolate chip–oatmeal cookie ice cream sandwiches

Bet you can't eat just one of these ice cream sandwiches. They are small oatmeal chocolate chip cookies half-coated in milk chocolate and filled with ice cream in a variety of flavors.

**mixing time** 20 minutes

**baking** 350° F. for about 12 minutes per batch

**cookies**

1 cup plus 2 tablespoons unbleached all-purpose flour

1/2 teaspoon baking soda

1/4 teaspoon salt

1/2 teaspoon ground cinnamon

10 tablespoons (1 1/4 sticks) unsalted butter, at room temperature

3/4 cup packed dark brown sugar

1/4 cup granulated sugar

1 large egg

1 teaspoon vanilla extract

1 3/4 cups oatmeal (not quick-cooking)

1 cup (5 3/4 ounces) milk chocolate chips

**coating**

1 1/2 cups (about 9 ounces) milk chocolate chips

1 1/2 tablespoons canola or corn oil

3/4 cup (3 ounces) finely chopped walnuts

1 pint total of assorted ice cream flavors (vanilla, coffee, chocolate, cherry vanilla, raspberry, mint chocolate chip, and/or strawberry)

**Make the cookies.** Position a rack in the middle of the oven. Preheat the oven to 350° F. Line 2 baking sheets with parchment paper.

Sift the flour, baking soda, salt, and cinnamon into a medium bowl and set aside.

In a large bowl, using an electric mixer on medium speed, beat the butter, brown sugar, and granulated sugar until smoothly blended, about 1 minute. Stop the mixer and scrape the sides of the bowl as needed during mixing. On low speed, add the egg and vanilla and mix until blended, about 1 minute. Add the flour mixture and oatmeal, mixing just until the flour is incorporated. Mix in the milk chocolate chips.

Drop heaping teaspoons of the dough onto the prepared baking sheets, spacing the cookies 1 inch apart. Bake the cookies one sheet at a time until the tops feel firm and the edges are lightly browned, about 12 minutes. Cool the cookies on the baking sheets for 5 minutes, then use a metal spatula to transfer the cookies to a wire rack to cool completely.

**Make the coating.** Arrange the cooled cookies on baking sheets. Put the milk chocolate chips and oil in a heatproof bowl or the top of a double boiler and place it over a saucepan of barely simmering water (or the bottom of the double boiler); the water should not touch the bowl. Stir until the chocolate is melted and smooth.

Use a small thin spatula to spread milk chocolate coating over half of the top of each cookie. Sprinkle the walnuts on the soft chocolate coating on half of the cookies. The walnuts will stick to the soft chocolate. Refrigerate the cookies to firm the chocolate. (The cookies can be wrapped tightly and stored in a tightly covered container in the freezer for up to 1 month. Do not defrost them before filling them with ice cream.)

Put a baking sheet or several pie pans in the freezer. Turn the cookies without the nuts bottom side up. Spread 1 tablespoon of ice cream on one of them, place a nut-topped cookie, nut side up, on the ice cream, and gently press the cookies together just to flatten the ice cream slightly. If you pair up the chocolate-coated halves so they are on the same side of the sandwich, it will be easier to pick up the sandwiches by the uncoated side, without melting the chocolate coating on your hands. Put the ice cream sandwich on the pan in the freezer. Continue filling and freezing the remaining cookies. Let the ice cream sandwiches freeze until firm, about 1 hour.

Wrap each sandwich in plastic wrap and seal the ice cream sandwiches in a plastic container or tin. Freeze for at least 5 hours, or up to 1 week.

Unwrap the ice cream sandwiches and serve.

# chocolate chip cookie-cookie dough ice cream bombe

This is an ice cream dessert made up of perfect pairs: Vanilla and chocolate for the ice cream, chocolate chip cookie dough and chocolate chip cookie pieces to mix in and top the bombe. Can't beat those combinations.

When baking a batch of Chock-Full of Chocolate Chip Cookies, cool, wrap, and freeze six cookies to use for this bombe.

**mixing time** 15 minutes

**dough**

5 tablespoons unsalted butter, at
 room temperature

½ cup packed light brown sugar

6 tablespoons granulated sugar

⅛ teaspoon salt

1 tablespoon water

1 teaspoons vanilla extract

¾ cup unbleached all-purpose flour

⅔ cup (4 ounces) miniature semisweet
 chocolate chips

2 pints vanilla ice cream, softened just
 until spreadable

1 pint chocolate ice cream, softened
 just until spreadable

**fudge sauce** (makes about 1¾ cups)

1 cup heavy whipping cream

2 tablespoons unsalted butter

2 cups (12 ounces) semisweet
 chocolate chips

1 teaspoon vanilla extract

6 Chock-Full of Chocolate Chip Cookies
 (page 24), crushed into small pieces

**continued...**

**Make the dough.** In a large bowl, using an electric mixer on medium speed, beat the butter, brown sugar, granulated sugar, and salt until smoothly blended, about 1 minute. Stop the mixer and scrape the sides of the bowl as needed during mixing. Add the water and vanilla and mix until blended. On low speed, add the flour, mixing just until it is incorporated. Mix in the chocolate chips. Set aside.

Chill a deep 2-quart bowl or metal mold with a round bottom in the freezer for 15 minutes. Line the bowl with plastic wrap, letting the wrap extend over the edge of the bowl. Use an ice cream spade or the back of a spoon to cover the bottom and sides of the bowl with the vanilla ice cream, leaving a cavity in the center for the chocolate ice cream. Reserve about one-third of the cookie dough, and scatter teaspoon-size pieces of the remaining dough over the ice cream. Spread the chocolate ice cream in the center cavity, scattering teaspoon-size bits of the remaining cookie dough into the ice cream as you spread it. Smooth the top. Cover tightly with plastic wrap and freeze until firm, at least 5 hours or up to 5 days.

**Make the fudge sauce.** In a medium saucepan, heat the cream and butter over low heat until the cream is hot and the butter melts. The mixture should form tiny bubbles and register about 175° F. on an instant-read thermometer; do not let the mixture boil, or it may form a skin on top. (If this does happen, use a spoon to carefully lift off the skin and discard it.) Remove the pan from the heat, add the chocolate chips, and let them sit in the hot cream mixture for about 30 seconds to soften. Add the vanilla and whisk until all of the chocolate is melted and the sauce is smooth.

Unmold the bombe at least 1 hour before serving it. Before unmolding it, chill a serving plate for about 15 minutes.

Remove the bombe from the freezer and unwrap it. Place the chilled serving plate on top of the bombe and invert. Release the bombe from the bowl by pulling on the ends of the plastic wrap, and remove the bowl. Discard the paper liner. Press the crushed cookies firmly over the outside of the bombe. Drizzle about ¼ cup of the fudge sauce over the cookies.

Return the bombe to the freezer for at least 1 hour or overnight. Cool, cover, and refrigerate the remaining fudge sauce. Reheat it over low heat before serving.

To serve, remove the bombe from the freezer and use a large sharp knife to cut it into 8 slices. Pass the remaining fudge sauce to pour over each serving.

# mail-order sources

**Buchanan Hollow Nut Company**

6510 Minturn Road
Le Grand, CA 95333

(800) 532-1500
FAX (209) 389-4321
www.bhnc.com

Nuts and dried fruit.

**L'Epicerie**

(866) 350-7575
www.lepicerie.com

Baking equipment and ingredients,
including high-quality miniature white
and dark chocolate chips, and peeled
roasted hazelnuts.

**King Arthur Flour Baker's Catalogue**

P.O. Box 876
Norwich, VT 05055

(800) 827-6836
FAX (800) 343-3002
www.kingarthurflour.com

Baking ingredients and equipment,
including unbleached all-purpose flour,
dried fruits, and peeled hazelnuts.

**Penzeys Spices**

P.O. Box 924
193000 W. Janacek Court
Brookfield, WI 53008-0924

(800) 741-7787
FAX (262) 785-7678
www.penzeys.com

Complete selection of high-quality
spices, including extra-fancy Vietnamese
cassia cinnamon and extracts.

**Williams-Sonoma**

P.O. Box 7456
San Francisco, CA 94120

(800) 541-2233
FAX (702) 363-2541
www.williams-sonoma.com

Baking equipment and ingredients.

# index

# table of equivalents

*The exact equivalents in the following tables have been rounded for convenience.*

## liquid/dry measurements

| u.s. | metric |
|---|---|
| ¼ teaspoon | 1.25 milliliters |
| ½ teaspoon | 2.5 milliliters |
| 1 teaspoon | 5 milliliters |
| 1 tablespoon (3 teaspoons) | 15 milliliters |
| 1 fluid ounce (2 tablespoons) | 30 milliliters |
| ¼ cup | 60 milliliters |
| ⅓ cup | 80 milliliters |
| ½ cup | 120 milliliters |
| 1 cup | 240 milliliters |
| 1 pint (2 cups) | 480 milliliters |
| 1 quart (4 cups, 32 ounces) | 960 milliliters |
| 1 gallon (4 quarts) | 3.84 liters |
| | |
| 1 ounce (by weight) | 28 grams |
| 1 pound | 454 grams |
| 2.2 pounds | 1 kilogram |

## oven temperature

| fahrenheit | celsius | gas |
|---|---|---|
| 250 | 120 | ½ |
| 275 | 140 | 1 |
| 300 | 150 | 2 |
| 325 | 160 | 3 |
| 350 | 180 | 4 |
| 375 | 190 | 5 |
| 400 | 200 | 6 |
| 425 | 220 | 7 |
| 450 | 230 | 8 |
| 475 | 240 | 9 |
| 500 | 260 | 10 |

## lengths

| u.s. | metric |
|---|---|
| ⅛ inch | 3 millimeters |
| ¼ inch | 6 millimeters |
| ½ inch | 12 millimeters |
| 1 inch | 2.5 centimeters |